Gateway
to a
Vast World

THE CHRONICLES OF TAO

The Wandering Taoist

Seven Bamboo Tablets of the Cloudy Satchel

Gateway to a Vast World

GATEWAY
TO A
VAST
WORLD

•

DENG MING-DAO

•

Portraits by
KWAN SAIHUNG

HARPER & ROW, PUBLISHERS
San Francisco

New York, Cambridge, Philadelphia, St. Louis
London, Singapore, Sydney, Tokyo

Designer: Mark Ong

FIRST EDITION

Library of Congress Cataloging-in-Publication Data

Deng, Ming-Dao
  Gateway to a vast world.

  Third book of the author's trilogy, the first of which is The
wandering Taoist, the second, Seven bamboo tablets of the
cloudy satchel.

  1. Kwan, Saihung. 2. Taoists—China—Biography. I. Kwan,
Saihung. II. Title.
BL1940.K93D44 1989   299'.514'0924 [B]   88-45656
ISBN 0-06-250230-1 (pbk.)

91 92 93 MCN 10 9 8 7 6 5 4 3 2

For My Classmates

Contents

Notes and Acknowledgments   ix

 O N E
Beyond Immortality   1

T W O
Contemplating the Void   29

T H R E E
The Hairpin   39

F O U R
Chinese of Pittsburgh   47

F I V E
The End of Huashan   72

S I X
No Song to Sing   92

S E V E N
Child of Peace   120

E I G H T
Isle of Anonymity   137

NINE
Golden Gloves   153

TEN
Gate of Liberation   182

ELEVEN
Perseverance   204

Afterword   217

Notes and Acknowledgments

This is the final book in a series with *The Wandering Taoist* and *Seven Bamboo Tablets of the Cloudy Satchel*. The trilogy comprises the *Chronicles of Tao*, and details the life of my Taoist teacher, Kwan Saihung. The first book deals with some of the training he received as a boy. The second one tells both of the dangers of a spiritual life as well as the necessity of transcending written orthodoxy. This last book tells of his struggles in a foreign culture, isolated from his master and his homeland.

These books are neither allegory nor fiction, but I have changed minor details in the narrative, as well as personal names, for the sake of privacy. At the same time, I have had to face the difficulty of communicating Chinese words for which there are no ready translations. I have employed various systems of phonetics if it seemed that such a practice would enhance recognition, though the primary system of romanization in this book is pinyin.

This book benefitted from the criticism of many people. I was fortunate to have the excellent comments of Elizabeth Kalashnikoff, Jade Snow Wong, and Mark Salzwedel. Peggy Gee made a great contribution in typing many parts of the manuscript.

Mr. Kwan, of course, provided the substance of this book through his recollections and dramatic tales. We met at odd times—Sunday afternoons, late nights—to rough out the various stories that would form the basis of this book, though the whole is actually pieced out of years of listening to him and watching him. I also gathered a great deal of material when Mr. Kwan and I went to Pittsburgh and New York. Naturally, this stimulated his memory even more, and allowed me to see some of the places he lived firsthand. This book is thus the result of our travels together.

ONE

Beyond Immortality

Late spring snow swirled around Kwan Saihung as he climbed the steep forest trail. Old pines cradled thick layers of ice on their green-needled boughs, barren branches of leafless trees were like smoke in the gorges. He looked through the diaphanous mists above him. Rock cliffs burnished by centuries of winter melt rose to nearly vertical heights, but he could not see their summit. They were obscured in storm cloud.

He began his climb up the cliffs. Soon, Saihung could pull himself up only with the help of heavy iron chains spiked into the hard granite, or by holding knotted ropes that had frozen stiff. The gloves on his hands stuck to the icy links, and they did not keep the cold from chilling his fingers. A harsh wind sometimes pushed him onto the stone. He reached repeatedly for narrow ledges, climbed carefully over hand-hewn steps contoured with ice.

At one point, he came to depressions in the rock. These indentations, packed with snow and a few maple leaves that had melted silhouette recesses, were believed to be the imprints of ox hooves made when Lao Tzu had renounced the world to ride westward. Now Kwan Saihung also felt his distance from ordinary society as he scaled the seven-thousand-foot towers of stone. He was leaving behind years of travel to enter the rarified world of a sacred Taoist sanctuary.

He stood for a moment at the top of the first one thousand steps, his chest heaving for oxygen at the higher altitude. Looking through the snow, he could barely make out the distant farmlands of the Shaanxi plains. As he climbed higher the enfolding parapets obscured all details that the ocean of mists did not. Ordinary life was insignificant from this spiritual citadel. There was only the pure tranquility of the mountain, the incomparable silence, the relieving calm. Troubles and tribulation seemed far away, worldly involvement was gone.

The cold air was sweet, clean, tangible. Saihung filled his lungs hungrily, greedily, though the freezing atmosphere dried his lips and hurt his throat. Each exhalation changed the breath within him, washed away the stagnant smoke of human society. It was wonderful to be back. His body relaxed, his soul opened like a flower. He felt safe, serene, and happy.

Wrapped in layers of quilted cotton clothes, a cloth cap tied around his head, and wearing straw-bottomed shoes, he tried to ignore the bone-chilling cold. The thrill of being on the mountain overran his senses. He hiked beside streams so clear that they would have been invisible save for their ripples. Icicles that hung like slender crystal spikes caught his eye as they shimmered on swaying branches. He watched a few maple leaves, thin and brown from being frozen all winter, float from rounded rock down into veridian pools. The water rushed sharply over the gray rock, the jade green liquid becoming a thousand shining swords. Saihung imagined his own body as clear and subtle as the water. He let his mind grow tranquil, immersed it in the frothing sublimity of the pool's color. In the world of men he was restless and competitive. In the forest quiet, beside the living stream, his soul found release and joy.

Five years ago he had lived here as a mountain hermit. Now in his thirties, he was a wanderer returning home.

No matter how wild the trajectory his life had taken, his center was Huashan. This mountain consecrated wholly to Taoism since the Tang dynasty was his enchanted peak.

At the age of nine he had been sent to live there by his family. He had not liked the poverty of monasticism at first, for he had been born to an aristocracy so privileged that it was a secret caste to the majority of Chinese and certainly to the Western world. His clan was fabulously wealthy, and even as a child he had had a sense of his privilege as a nobleman. But he had met a Taoist accidentally, and this single incident diverted him from the path he might have taken as a member of his family. His teacher, the Grand Master of Huashan, had seen the potential for spirituality. He had accepted Saihung as the thirteenth and last disciple of a sect of warrior-priest Taoists. This sect had its roots in the antiquity of China's earliest dynasties, when holy men and warriors were not seen as separate ideals.

He had entered a community comprised of both mature spiritual aspirants and hundreds of boys sent for parochial educations. Most graduates entered secular life, or became priests in communities eager to have prestigious seminarians. Others stayed as monks, often for a reason other than the pure motivation of renunciation. They wanted to get an education, learn a trade, flee the pain of broken homes or lost loves, retire from military careers, or perhaps even abandon criminal life. That was a radical enough choice. The options in pre-Republican China were few, and the educated normally chose between scholarly and military endeavors. Entering a spiritual community was frowned upon, for the aspirant was then considered useless in a material world. Saihung's parents had only intended that he receive a high-level education and had formally disowned him when he had taken priestly vows.

The Grand Master, both the head of his sect and abbot of the entire mountain, had guided Saihung's own education with patience and care. He had assigned his own personal acolytes as tutors to oversee Saihung's progress, and he himself designed each new stage of Saihung's life. He designated Saihung as a vehicle to receive a grand religious tradition, but he intended that his student learn more than the beliefs and spartan practices of the lineage. He also decreed that the boy be educated in every other conceivable art and discipline. Other monks, nearly grotesque in their divine and eccentric abilities, had taught him scriptures, classics, poetry, painting, herbalism, massage, acupuncture, music, martial arts, and meditation. Each of his teachers sought to make him a paragon that they had either once been themselves or had abandoned hope of ever becoming. He had been selected as someone special, to be cloistered until he fulfilled his potential.

The influence of his teachers showed in every part of his being. He was brawny, not tall, but strong enough to have earned the nickname "Steel Lion." Saihung was poised, alert, exhibiting a combination of martial confidence and priestly dignity. He became all that the masters might have hoped; and though he qualified to be their champion, he was headstrong. He had intermittently forsaken the temple to throw himself into the uncertainty of changing times. China's collision with the West had shattered its brittle ancient culture, had broken the royal world, and had forced an abandonment of poetic standards for a driving, nationalistic lust for modernity. That change excited him.

He had been fortunate that his master had understood him to the core. It was said that a true master-student relationship represented a mystical link. It was unorthodox for a monk to go in and out of temple life, but his master was wise enough to defy tradition when necessary. When the elders of the White Cloud Monastery, the highest Taoist governing power, had tried to force Saihung into the priesthood at the age of twenty, it was Saihung's master who had stood before them to tear their decree to pieces. "He is my student," his master had said. "I will not force him into this role."

Saihung then left monastic life, leaving facets of his personality incompletely organized. Aristocrat, warrior, ascetic, youth: each of these represented a conflict with either family or religious hierarchy. He eased that tension by wandering. Accompanying an uncle who was a wealthy fur trader, or going alone by bicycle, he had toured Germany, France, and Eastern Europe, even though World War II was in progress. He found charm and beauty wherever he went, and had taken sentimental likings to the Black Forest, bridges over the Danube, the sound of Chopin. He loved to stay in alpine villages, and appreciated the hospitality that people proffered even to strangers. Though the land had been devastated, he took it all in, and the enchantment of a foreign land was mixed with the enthusiasm of his youth. For a time, he had even wanted to move to Europe, but his only friends were members of an aristocracy dying everywhere. They could offer him no solace.

Saihung returned to China. He was studying at Yenching University as the People's Republic came into being in 1949. An essay he had written caught the eye of Premier Zhou Enlai, who habitually recruited aides from the schools. Zhou summoned him, discussed ideas with him, and invited him to travel. Little by little, he assigned minor responsibilities to Saihung, covertly watching how the young man acted. Only when Zhou was satisfied that Saihung was a potential asset did he invite him to become

one of his many undersecretaries. This role was classically
Chinese. Saihung had gone through an initiation ritual in
which he had ceremoniously knelt down to become
Zhou's disciple.

Saihung proved to be an excellent and ruthless politician. Before long he was sitting in the People's Congress—
a pale, severe, calculating figure in a gray Mao suit—
studying the results of stratagems he had created. Being
a part of government, as Zhou taught him, meant the absolute use of power. Allies had to be cultivated, enemies
had to be contained or destroyed. For one trained since
childhood to be a martial artist, being cruel in politics was
simple. He loved to anticipate the actions of his rivals,
set up circumstances to thwart them. He enjoyed their
squirming.

Cunning and brutal manipulations were matter-of-fact
necessities in politics. All would have been fine had Saihung not had another side to him. Whether innate or fos-
tered by the monastery, he had a conscience and emotion.
These two factors were as much a part of him as his ability to wield power, and they were liabilities for a politician. He brooded about his actions; sometimes he secretly
sympathized with his victims.

He left the government in 1951. The danger of political
intrigue, rivalry with Zhou's other disciples, and disen-
chantment with the impermanence of political reform
were the outward reasons that he left. But the more true
reasons were the tensions between his mercenary and sensitive sides. He could never bring himself to complete the
ultimate act of power: the eradication of his compassion.

Saihung had remained a solitary man, troubled by his
inner schism and uncertain about his own destiny. He
wanted, if not peace, at least a way through his dilemmas.
Only when the futility of his life of travel had worn him

down, and his dangerous ambivalence about public life had become too prominent, did he remember the recluse who had raised him. His longing snapped into focus. He decided that he would return to learn the higher stages of Taoism.

For as long as he had traveled, he had never discovered the possibility of learning such secrets elsewhere. It was said that deepening meditative techniques would teach extraordinary, even supernatural things. He wanted to soar into heaven, dive into hell, know all things seen and unseen. He wanted to increase his health and take it to the ultimate extreme of longevity.

The Taoists were famous for utilizing esoteric practices: breath control; concentration of the mind; stretching, contracting, and twisting the body; techniques of hygiene; and compounding unusual herbal elixirs in order to prolong their lives. Originally these practices were developed because immortality was seen as desirable for its own sake. Only after generations of holy men had made their experiments and drawn conclusions did the quest for immortality reach the belief that the Grand Master now held: Longevity was worthwhile only to allow the practitioner to exhaust thoroughly his exploration of the Tao. For Saihung, that exploration of the Tao was very personal. He was not so much interested in it for abstract philosophical speculation, as much as he desired a simple way to understand himself. He wanted to learn the wisdom that would unify his personality.

The Taoist life was not glorious. It was all homespun cloth, patched robes, bleached wood, dusty brick, coarse gruel. Governments were never patrons, for a Taoist, even at best, was the least cooperative of all holy men. Patrons found the doctrines as abstruse as the peaks were difficult to ascend. Gods had no gold for the Taoists, and the real fact was that "renunciation" only existed as long as there were others willing to support such efforts. Few on the outside had any emotion for the dwellers of Huashan save for scorn, condescension, or superstitious fear. But spiritual richness still flourished in surroundings of poverty.

The monks that he saw as he passed the Gate of Southern Heaven were a testimonial to the rigorous and disciplined men who found vitality in the harsh surroundings. Huashan was a little like a university, except that there was a quietness to the way people moved back and forth, a seriousness of intent on their faces. The younger ones were dressed in blue or gray, the older monks in black. He passed dozens of men who were either working or hurrying to classes. As mountain ascetics, each one was to attune himself to the change in the sky, the stillness of the mountain, the compassion of the earth, the ferocity of thunder, and the meditation of the lake.

Saihung crossed a rustic log bridge over a pouring cataract and began his final ascent up the South Peak. As he came closer to his master, he began climbing in greater excitement. Through a cleft in the mighty granite, above the tops of pines with trunks like bronze, he saw his master's temple. It floated like a dream in the falling snow, its black tile roof frosted white. He could see priests standing at the top of the trail, men he had known all his life. There was no embracing, no shouts of joy or welcome. He walked back into his home temple in solemn quiet. He could only bring his left palm to his heart—the thumb touching his chest, the fingers upright—in the gesture of greeting.

As he walked up the stone steps and into the dark gate of the shrine, he met Mist Through a Grove and Sound of Clear Water, the two monks who had helped rear him. Now in their forties, the two returned his bow deeply. As they stood upright, they performed a series of hand gestures that formed a secret sign of their sect. Saihung replied in kind, but the two men began giggling. By the time they were finished, they were overcome with mirth.

Saihung was annoyed. Here he had climbed seven thousand feet in anticipation of a homecoming, and he was being laughed at.

"You're not supposed to laugh in the temple," he whispered to them.

Saihung's reproach proved even more hilarious to them. His two older brothers looked at his dishevelled appearance, the hat askew on his head, and his pants soaked from snow and the spray of streams.

"You're not supposed to come into the temple like that either," laughed Sound of Clear Water. He was a tall, beardless man seldom given even to smiling.

Saihung pulled the hat angrily from his head. The acolytes only laughed all the more: Though his hair was short, it seemed as if every single strand was plastered down in a different direction.

"You'd better arrange yourself before you see the Grand Master," admonished Mist Through a Grove. Saihung bridled immediately. He wondered if he would always be a child to his older classmates.

"I'll bathe right away," he said with all the dignity he could muster.

"Impossible," said Sound of Clear Water. "The showers are closed until evening."

Saihung was about to burst out in frustration when he heard the familiar voice of his master.

"It's of no consequence," said the Grand Master.

Saihung turned in the hall to see his master with two other elderly priests. They were apparently on their way from a discussion. The acolytes withdrew two steps in deference. Saihung bowed immediately by kneeling and touching his head repeatedly to the tile floor. He did not care that he was leaving a puddle from the water and sweat on his head.

Stroking his beard thoughtfully, the Grand Master greeted Saihung with a formal phrase. Beyond that utterance, his master acted as if he had not been gone at all. The Grand Master told Saihung to rise. For a minute, he looked deeply into his student's eyes. Saihung felt that his own thoughts had been interrupted. He could only stare back, mesmerized.

His master was over six feet tall—thin, and sturdy as a pine. He seemed ancient, though no one knew his true age. His often half-lidded eyes came to upsweeping corners as sharp as the tip of a writing brush. The mouth was thin-lipped and closed in priestly silence. His jaw was firm, the nose like a wedge, his forehead proud and high. The coil of hair at the crown and the thick white beard were like fine strands of silver wire against somber black robes. His skin was brown from years of living on exposed and lonely mountaintops. Fine wrinkles from wearisome responsibilities wove a net around his quiet eyes. His gaze was steady, and expressed deep knowledge, understanding, and benevolence. Saihung saw a hint of sadness, a trace of resignation. He always wondered whether this was regret for the past, or an acceptance of a future as yet unknown.

The Grand Master stretched his hand forward in blessing. He assigned temple tasks and a demanding regimen of contemplation as if Saihung had never been gone. "From this day forth, it will be your task to solve the mystery of the self," said the Grand Master. "You will find Sound of Clear Water and ask him to assign you to

*The Grand Master of Huashan
wearing the distinctive hat of his office.*

a meditation hut. You must answer this question for me: Do you exist?"

Saihung looked up at the master. What an odd question, he thought to himself. But he had little time to think about it just then, and he could not ask for further explanation. The Grand Master smiled slightly before he gestured to the acolytes to follow him. They left Saihung alone in the hall.

Turning into the darkness, Saihung saw the image of the Queen Mother of the West, one of Huashan's patron deities. He walked up to the altar and offered incense. It felt good to be back.

In the ensuing days, Saihung returned to his classes and began to work on repairing the North Peak Temple. The weight of snow had broken several places in the tile roof and the repairs could not wait until spring. Balancing precariously on ladders, he and other monks took advantage of a clear day to carry tiles up and cement them in place. It was a dizzying task, for the north peak was a narrow wedge of stone several thousand feet in height. The temple was situated astride the saddle-like ridge, and a fall would have sent him plunging.

The high vantage point allowed him a wonderful view. As he scanned the valley below, he noticed a strange flash of metal. He had his duties to perform, but he was curious. Telling the supervising monk that he had to relieve himself, Saihung walked through the brick temple and made his way carefully down the trail. The storm-whipped ridge was bald of trees. He was thankful to get out of the wind and into a forest.

Saihung came to a rise that was covered with pines. He could hear two men talking, but he could not see them from where he stood. Saihung walked carefully over the snow to avoid detection. As he crept closer, he was surprised to hear his master's voice.

"I am a renunciate who has lost all hankering for fame," said the Grand Master.

"I am also a priest," Saihung heard a deep voice reply. "But though the world of Tao is apart from the mortal world, there must nevertheless be distinctions between high and low."

"Tragic indeed that you should take such a view," murmured the Grand Master. "True followers of the way do not care about their place in any hierarchy."

"You speak as the abbot of Huashan. Isn't that contradictory?"

"My office is merely a duty. I would forsake it if required."

"But the person remains who he is."

"For as long as my destiny lasts."

"It is the person that I seek, after all, not the empty identity. It is against you that I have come to test my skill."

Saihung could not help but inch closer to gain a view. There in a snow-covered clearing, he could see his master, but not the man with whom he was speaking. Conifers stood starkly in the snow, black rocks protruded from the white banks.

The Grand Master turned slightly. Saihung saw that he was holding a sword of brilliant steel. A long tassel of white horsehair was tied to the handle.

"I am a simple and direct man," said the Grand Master. "What use is it to duel with me? It will surely not add to your prestige to best someone my age."

The other man laughed. "I am a Taoist. I do not care for prestige. I only care about self-perfection. Your modesty is as admirable as it is inaccurate. You are one of the few true swordsmen left."

"Why not say the truth?" returned the Grand Master. "You are trying to discredit Huashan and usurp power for yourself."

There was a tense pause. The Grand Master must have known the man's true motivation, thought Saihung. He cautiously moved to see him.

He was surprised to see a dwarf. Dressed in the gray robes of a Taoist priest, with white beard and topknot, he seemed almost as old as the Grand Master. His head was large, and though his eyes were somewhat crooked, they still came to the sharp corners that were supposed to signify a man of intelligence. He was only tall enough to come to the Grand Master's waist, but his hands were large and powerful. The sword he held was unusually long. Nearly four feet in length, it was a blade of purple steel, a metal famous throughout the martial world for its flexible strength. His tassel was dyed black and red. The dwarf showed no emotion at the Grand Master's accusation. He only brought his blade before him in silent challenge.

"All fighting, whether by swordsmen, sorcerers, or gods themselves, is egotism," declared the Grand Master.

"Your wisdom was gained through contest," said the dwarf. "I crave the experience of testing myself against you."

"Must you?" asked the Grand Master. "Acts of power are acts of greed."

"Only one who has power sermonizes about greed," replied the dwarf testily. "I have not yet gained what I must. You bar my way."

"Sad . . . sad indeed that you should be so bitter."

"Sadness is an emotion. A good swordsman has no emotion."

"You believe that you are such a swordsman?"

"There is only one way to answer," said the dwarf, thrusting the point of his blade forward. The tip began to tremble with the energy he projected through it.

"Even when one renounces the world, trouble will still come," sighed the Grand Master upon seeing this aggressive gesture. "You are determined to go through with this?"

"Yes," replied the dwarf. "My honor is at stake."

"May you someday see how useless honor is," replied the Grand Master. "But since you will not relent, I must respond. As your fame precedes you, I will not lighten my stroke."

"Nor will I."

The two men were about twenty feet apart. As a prelude, each was allowed to go through a few saluting postures emblematic of their style. The dwarf brought his sword before him, circled his free arm with a flourish, and made several cuts and parries. His open hand was held in the sword gesture, a closed hand with only the index and second fingers extended. He ended his salute first by pointing his fingers at the Grand Master, then by levelling the tip of his blade straight at his opponent's heart.

It was the Grand Master's turn, and he ritualistically went through his own salute. He brought the sword across his chest, raised it high, crouched down into a low stance, and leapt up onto one leg before settling into a position of readiness. He also pointed his weapon straight to the heart. Like his opponent's sword, the tip of the Grand Master's sword began to vibrate from the force conducted through the razor sharp steel. The dwarf scoffed.

"Green Dragon Sword style," he spat out, for he recognized the Grand Master's postures. "A rather common style!"

The Grand Master remained silent. There was a moment of utter stillness, each swordsman waiting for the other to commit himself first. Snow began falling again, and the flakes caught on the bare steel.

The dwarf charged with a loud shout. His legs were mighty and he leapt high in the air at the Grand Master. Without moving his stance, the Grand Master bent over backward to dodge the cut. His waist was so flexible that he sprang back right away and then twisted around toward his opponent. The blade just missed, but it kept the dwarf from counterattacking.

Saihung knew that the sign of expert swordsmen was that they never clashed their swords directly with one another. To block was a sign of poor skill. Rather, the best fighters were always able to avoid the other's weapon, no matter how swift the combat.

The Grand Master came with a downward thrust, but his opponent easily sidestepped, aiming directly at the outstretched wrist. The Grand Master turned smoothly in a circular parry and hacked downward. The dwarf dodged and thrust at the chin. Each fighter took skillful, nearly balletic poses—at one point, the Grand Master dropped into a full split, the dwarf leapt into the air like a whirlwind—as they both tried to gain an opening. But it was not easy. Saihung could see that the dwarf actually had an advantage because of his quickness and his height. The Grand Master was forced to turn wider circumferences to escape return thrusts.

The dwarf jumped up again, his body spinning rapidly. He was like a hurtling comet. His sword moved so swiftly that Saihung could not see it. He could only hear it slicing the air in a terrifying sound halfway between a tearing sheet and a shriek. The Grand master spun, pausing abruptly behind his attacker. His movement was fierce, his blade accelerating past the range of visibility as he twisted it out.

The dwarf parried, opening the Grand Master's guard for a moment. He could not turn his blade in time, so he smashed the butt of his handle toward the Grand Master's heart. The Grand Master jumped to the side in a spinning hack that the dwarf dodged only by twisting his whole body in the air.

Brief flashes of steel seemed to fly out from centrifugal force. Saihung knew that their spinning movements, characteristic of high swordsmanship, were not wholly a consequence of muscular or acrobatic abilities. Both men had brought power gained from years of meditative cultivation into play. Internal energy moved in spirals and lightened their bodies, and this was why they leapt and turned in the drifting snowflakes.

This was the true meaning of their contest. Thrusting and parrying were secondary. Strategy and martial experience were only remotely relevant. What was being tested was their totalities as men, their attainment of internal energy. There were thirteen levels to swordsmanship, with the first level already hopelessly above the average knight. The two fighters were already in the higher echelons of this elite. For them, swords were mere extensions of their bodies, and their bodies were mere instruments. They were throwing soul against soul, using the utmost of their inner fires.

Finally, the dwarf lunged low and cut the Grand Master's thigh. The Grand Master dropped down, feigning a serious wound. As his opponent came in for the kill, the Grand Master turned and cut off the dwarf's topknot. He could just have easily cut lower. The dwarf hesitated a moment, and in that second, the Grand Master stuck him in the wrist. The sword fell to the rock with a sound like an iron ingot hitting the foundry floor. It lay immobile and dark in the snow: an effigy corpse for its master. The Grand Master leapt up and raised his blade heavenward, but the now frightened dwarf ran away. Saihung's master did nothing to pursue him.

It was wrong for Saihung to have watched the fight. Duels were a private matter, not an affair for gawkers. He stole away, apprehensive of punishment. He guessed that his master might have been aware of his presence, but Saihung decided to say nothing if his master remained quiet about it. He hurried back to his duties at the North Peak Temple.

"How could one go so far and long to relieve oneself?" demanded the supervisor. He was a middle-aged priest with a military bearing.

"It was a matter of the 'large convenience,' " said Saihung with an exaggerated stammer.

"One should not use such vernacular in the presence of the gods," said the priest hastily. Now Saihung had doubled his offense.

"This insignificant one recognizes his sin," apologized Saihung. "Please relent, though I deserve punishment."

"It is of little consequence," said the priest. "Go back to your duties."

Saihung went back to carrying tiles, but as he swayed in the wind, he relished the memory of his teacher's fight.

The Grand Master summoned Saihung two days later. His master did not limp from the cut, and he made no reference to his duel. The Grand Master merely nodded to Saihung and gestured toward the monastery gate. The two of them walked toward the crest of the South Peak, quiet and yet aware of each other.

"Asceticism is possible only away from people," commented the Grand Master as they came to the very edge of a high cliff. "Can't you feel it?"

Saihung nodded as he felt the sting of the wind. There wasn't a bit of humanity in sight, only pure nature stretching to the horizon. He felt aloof from all that was normally considered important. After years of training, he had come to the conclusion that perceptions were superior to doctrine and procedure.

"Only here, away from the pull of other minds, can one attain tranquility," continued the Grand Master. "Tranquility leads to stillness. In stillness there is the possibility of wisdom."

"You've said that meditation is the key," said Saihung, anticipating his master's favorite theme.

"But not simply meditation. Life is not simplistic. Tao changes. Our methods to know it must also have variety. Live your life with discipline and explore relentlessly. Do not limit yourself, even by meditation."

"Then why do you preach a life of restriction?"

"This enforces discipline. Self-indulgence is a liability. Tao is known by the free. Only the disciplined are free to chase the flow. Eternal flux rules the universe. Know the Tao by inaction. That is the way to know its secrets. Keep to action. That is the way to experience its outcome."

" 'Be desireless to know the essence of Tao. Have desire to know its manifestations,' " said Saihung, quoting from scripture.

"Yes," responded the Grand Master. "But you should speak from your own experience. Quoting holy words is useless. They only point back on oneself. They all say 'Look within.' The only real value lies in firsthand experience."

His master was tough, admitted Saihung admiringly. The Grand Master had a taste for severity and discipline.

Longevity was simply a procedure to extend the process of simplifying the personality through penance and self-sacrifice. It was pure drudgery, a life of restriction meant to force the explosion of human potential by sheer compression. They walked further on and stood for a minute at another ridge. Small trees, stunted by the bitter climate, dotted the pristine stone sporadically. Stronger trees stood starkly against the gray heavens.

"Look! Look!" urged the Grand Master. "Do you need a book? Look! Feel! The Tao surrounds you!"

There before them a vast panorama of aged peaks, their edges still proudly sharp and lofty even after centuries, stretched to the horizon. They were like many dragons, the rising mist like a swirling surf. Snow frosted the tops of the mountains where the aerial tide had ebbed. Clouds swept through like charging armies. The wind came in gusts and shook the tortured sentinel pines. Nature was supreme, nature was pure. It changed constantly, its transformations surrounded them.

Huashan dwarfed the puny men who stood so insignificantly on its ledges. They were nothing here. Their aspirations were mere glimmers, their bodies stupidly fragile. Their lifespans were only moments in infinity. They stood in their transitoriness; master and disciple who were like footnotes to the epic of heaven and earth.

"Knowing the Tao is essential," said the Grand Master. He turned toward Saihung and smiled reassuringly. "Meditation is the way to know the Tao. Please tell me what progress you've made."

"I am not sure . . . the question that you posed to me is not easy to answer."

"What is so hard?" returned the Grand Master gently. "The question was only three words long."

"That's true. I have been meditating on it since my return. Nevertheless . . ."

"I will restate it," said his master. "I simply asked you: Do you exist?"

Saihung was silent. Somehow, he felt that he would say the wrong thing no matter what his response.

The Grand Master urged him on. "Are you speechless? You who are so fond of debating and arguing? You who have been to the university and traveled far and wide? Answer! Answer!"

"Yes!" burst out Saihung. "I exist!"

"Do you? Then where is your self? Show it to me."

"Why, I am right here before you."

"Are you? Are you so sure that I exist?"

"Master!" exclaimed Saihung. "Yes!"

"But I have no self to show you."

"I see you," said Saihung. He wondered if his master was getting senile.

"You see only a body, a borrowed vessel."

Saihung looked at his master in an effort to understand what was being presented to him. The Grand Master's life of deep cultivation had worked his face into eccentric beauty. Both the warrior and scholar showed, and tensions between the two extremes were resolved in the visage of the hermit. Did this man exist? For Saihung, he certainly did. The Grand Master had told him that he saw only a borrowed vessel. But of course, Saihung realized that there was more to the man than his outer shell. It wasn't hard to accept that he should not view a person merely by the body. Saihung was confident in his position. He would not be so dumb as to limit the self to the material and the physical. He took up the debate again.

"Of course there is something unseen, besides the body."

"What is that?" asked the Grand Master.

"The mind. The immortal soul. These exist. The scriptures tell us that there are three sheaths within us. The soul, the mind, and the body."

"You are a good schoolboy," said the Grand Master mockingly. "But I don't hear your own experience in those words."

"Master," replied Saihung in a patient tone, "I've meditated for years. I know the mind."

"If you knew the mind, you would not speak so recklessly. Those who truly understand the mind know that it is both friend and enemy. Don't you realize that it is the mind that subverts you?"

"The mind is real," declared Saihung.

"No, the mind is not real," responded the Grand Master with equal emphasis.

"I have seen too much of the mind's powers to accept that it is not real."

"Powers!" The Grand Master cut him off. "What have they done but obscured your true nature?"

Saihung felt irritated. He felt his teacher was being deliberately difficult—even hypocritical. The man had ten times Saihung's abilities, possessed skills bordering on the divine. It was ridiculous for him to suggest that powers were a hindrance. Saihung would have pounded any other man who had been so contrary.

But this was his master, and there was no possibility of hitting him. He was forced instead to consider what his master was saying. His master had referred to Saihung's true nature. He looked at himself for a clue.

He saw himself as a man who celebrated physicality. As a veteran of the Sino-Japanese war, he had staked his life on bone and sinew. He had been sickly in his youth— his mother had spent enough for ten families' fortunes on rare and expensive medicines—and there was something in his hardened and barrel-chested stature that came from that early obsession with health. His upper arms were like other men's thighs, his legs were like tree trunks. His complexion was red, his face wide as a shield. His large eyes glistened and showed determination. His thick black hair grew quickly, which was good. He had cut it when he had left Huashan. Now he wanted to grow it long enough to again have a topknot.

Though he had spent years hardening his hands for fighting, the fingers were paradoxically long, tapered, and almost delicate. Looking at them, one might have expected a musician, a writer, or perhaps a privileged gentleman. Before the revolution he had indeed indulged in his aesthetic inclinations. He was well read—one of his hobbies was using his family's prestige and wealth to collect the manuscripts of famous authors—and he was a collector not only of antiquarian books, but of porcelain statues, antiques, and fine painting. He was a connoisseur of all ten of China's famous provincial cuisines, had a penchant for tailor-made clothes, and had savored life's finest offerings. The only pleasures he never indulged in because of his monastic upbringing and inherent shyness were wine, opium, and women.

The Grand Master had often made it clear that he thought Saihung's emphasis on physical might was foolish, not because of intellectual snobbery, but because he, the Grand Master, knew internal strength to be superior. He saw indulgence in aesthetic pleasure to be trivial—but only because he had once walked within the Imperial Palace itself. He felt Saihung's knowledge to be but a trickle, but only because he had already drunk an ocean's worth and still thirsted for more. This superiority actually made Saihung more reckless. He always felt that his master would keep him from making a disastrous mistake. This faith had given him the confidence to wander, and the more he had wandered, the more he had felt his own reality. Yes, he told himself. I have done much. I have seen much. I have experiences. I have memories.

"The mind is powerful," began Saihung again. "I know that it is not my body. Though I practice martial arts, I have also traveled outside my body. I have soared to other places, holding onto your sleeve. Don't you remember, master?"

"How trivial!" declared the Grand Master. "A few insignificant flights and you think that establishes the self? I see nothing impressive about a mere wisp of smoke flitting here and there."

"The mind is my true nature," responded Saihung stubbornly.

"And since you've learned a few mental circus tricks, you assume that you're explaining the self?"

"Well . . . yes."

"That merely traps you in your mind. Pursuing power and intellect, astral travel and clairvoyance—these only strengthen your trap."

"Then why did I learn them?"

"Because you are greedy for power. You should learn them to understand their uselessness. Know magic, shun magic."

Saihung refused to be bested in the discussion. He tried a new direction.

"What about the gods, whom we revere? Surely they exist." He knew his master was devout.

"Even worse!" The Grand Master refused to take the bait. "It may sound like blasphemy, but the gods are also trapped in their minds. They live for eternity clinging to their identities and their roles. The Jade Emperor is omnipotent, omniscient, omnipresent, and no more."

"No more?" interjected Saihung. "Can there be anything else?"

"Yes, there is something else. We Taoists believe that there is something besides the gods. The Jade Emperor is only one being. He is not all beings, and he is not the universe, or all universes. The gods, in this respect, are as pathetic as humans in their delight for powers. This is their limitation: They still believe in the self."

"Well, if scripture is not enough, my mind is not enough, even the gods are not enough, then there can be no Tao."

"You are wrong," said the Grand Master, finally fixing him with a steady gaze. "When there are no scriptures, there is no mind, and there are no gods, then there is Tao."

They were silent for a time. The Grand Master closed his eyes while Saihung stood awkwardly in the bone-numbing chill. This habit of closing his eyes in the middle of a conversation had always unnerved Saihung. He was never sure whether to stand there, or leave. As always, he decided to wait. This time, he considered himself lucky that the Grand Master began to speak after only an hour's lapse.

"Do you understand death?"

"I believe so," replied Saihung, as he tried to keep his teeth from chattering. He had seen many die during wars, famine, and in fights.

"Is death final, or is it merely a transformation?"

"The self of instinct decays with the body. The self of the mind and the soul are reincarnated," stated Saihung from his lessons. "If one practices spirituality, there is the potential to transcend death with one's individual awareness intact."

"Is that what you want?"

Of course it was. But he thought it best to be cautious in admitting it. "I have been taught that this was best."

"You are correct, but far off the mark. Your only concern should be liberation."

"Indeed it is."

"But liberation not just from life and death, transmigration, and one's own desires, liberation from one's own mind as well. The mind itself is capable of transcending death: We believe that one will go where one wills at the moment of death. Those who are confused will pass into oblivion or float in limbo: Sometimes they are not even aware that they have died. Others can, through the practice of good deeds and austerities, become gods. The majority, however, fall in between: Still clinging to a desire for life, or having been so unfulfilled, they come back again and again. Like the Butterfly Lovers, who were reincarnated sixty times before they could fulfill their love and gain release, the average person is repeatedly reincarnated to complete his destiny."

The Grand Master looked at Saihung. "All these people have something in common: They are prisoners of the mind. Whether they are the dunce too muddled to comprehend death or the sage who has been elevated to a god, they still cling to their identities. There is still something higher."

This aroused Saihung. The Grand Master knew his student well. Saihung would always reach for the best.

"The best is emptiness," said the Grand Master. "You must strive to be empty. Learn longevity, yes. But don't try to be immortal. Even gods die. Live long enough to fulfill your destiny."

"How does one do that?"

"By having a goal in life. Have a purpose and your life will be purposeful. Have a meaning and your life will be meaningful. Make a decision and stick to it, not dogmatically or rigidly. Persevere and be flexible. Once a goal has been selected, nothing else must interfere. Cut all that is ordinarily considered essential in order to find meaning. If one has a powerful motivation for living, then choices are clear-cut. With discipline, sacrifices are made for a higher goal, and one acts with confidence and directness. Then you will go into the source satisfied that you've completed your life on earth. Nothing will pull you back. You are free."

"Master, what is this source?"

"I will not tell you now. You must find out and tell me. Then I will know that you have truly found it."

They walked back toward the temple. The evening bells had begun to ring. Saihung continued to ponder his master's words. He had to rely on his faith in his master. He had been with his master long enough to catch minor mistakes, see him indulge in favorite foods, bear his moodiness and recalcitrance, recognize quotations from books, hear him fart and burp. But that wasn't enough to make the Grand Master any less of an authority to him. Others claimed to be devout because they never had their piety tested by all too human teachers, or prayed to altars that never responded, or based their allegiance on masters with whom they seldom had actual contact. Saihung maintained his allegiance because his master was a genuinely accomplished and human sage.

Taoism meant liberation from every shackle of socialization and materialism. It meant the transcendence of all that marked him as human. His master had told him to leave behind emotion, intellect, and the metaphysical stains on his soul that was karma. He was ultimately to question and scrutinize first the mind, then the soul itself, until it became formless, was perceived as empty. There was no heaven to hope for, no rewards of jewels and light. Taoism was not otherworldly. Everything was to be done during his lifetime, not postponed to some afterlife. All that there was to know could be known now. There were no grand promises. Only a humble and simple journey toward *wu wei*, nothingness. He would become nothing. In becoming nothingness, he would become Tao.

Tao was everything. Tao was limitless. Tao was the great mystery. It was to be known not by common means, but by mystical ones. It was to be known not by conducting exhaustive quantitative data, but by paring away one's interfering consciousness. It was not to be known by rigorous effort, but by subtle meditation. Tao was the dynamic flow of life that could not be opposed by any person, nor even the human race. Tao was like water; it accepted all without consciousness, achieved all without premeditation. It was the source that was beginning and end. Tao was constant change. It could not be isolated, it could not be calibrated. Permanency was stagnation. There could be no such thing as permanent realization. There was only following the Way.

Contemplating the Void

Saihung walked into the icy night, his way lit only by a paper lantern. His evening devotions were complete. In the remaining hour before midnight, he was to take advantage of the time when *yin* was at its height for his fourth meditation of the day. As he made his way toward his cell, he noticed the throw of golden light. He remembered the old saying: "The wise man who seeks the way carries a candle before him." That candle was supposed to be knowledge, but it only showed the way. One still had to walk step by step.

As a young novitiate, he had lived in dormitories with other boys. His present regimen of meditation required that he live alone in a small cottage. He had been assigned to a one-room place large enough only for a bed, table, and bookshelf. He was to live there until he made a break-through, and he had previously been sealed into such buildings for months. Only his teacher could visit, and all eating, study, and meditation was to be conducted in the tiny, solitary house perched on an undercut cliff.

Typically Taoist, the brick, wood, and tile hut was built on a ledge that was barely an aberration in the rock wall. Generations of monks had gained their realization in this fragile shelter, and it was said that years of such medi-tation had soaked into the very particles of the building. By opening his being in meditation, Saihung was to ride the reverberations of those people's enlightenment to the same states of consciousness.

The interior was of rustic plaster, whitewashed. A few scrolls of landscapes hung from the walls, but otherwise there was no decoration. The wooden eaves were exposed, gray and rough timbers barely stripped of bark. He hung a sign on the exterior that stated "meditation," so that he would remain undisturbed, and closed the pine door tightly against the wind. Taking a bundle of straw and kindling, he renewed the fire under his brick bed. Only layers of thick cotton quilting and the warm platform would prevent him from freezing during the night. He decided that it was too cold to undress; he would go to sleep fully clothed, with a hat tied to his head and a scarf over his nose.

He felt his hair by pushing his hand beneath his hat. It was shoulder length. Soon he would be able to pin it into the Taoist symbol. He went to a wooden trunk and took out a piece of silver. This hairpin was shaped like a straight blade about one-quarter-inch wide, narrowing over a six-inch length to a blunt tip. On one end was an intricately wrought dragon head.

He looked at the pin, topaz-colored in the lantern's light. It had a preciousness for him that went beyond its value as a metal. His master had given it to him when he had been initiated at the age of sixteen. No other person had ever touched this hairpin. It had been consecrated and bestowed personally, just as his spirituality had been sparked by personal transmission. He had worn it through years of asceticism and had kept it during years of travel. It was the symbol of his renunciation and a sign of the strength of Taoism. He put it away, looking forward to the day he would wear it.

Saihung took out a book and a fountain pen, to avoid the tedium of grinding ink and preparing paper. He wrote down all that he and his master had discussed that afternoon. He pondered the conversation with some anxiety. He did not quite understand all that the Grand Master was teaching him. In fact, he had a fearful doubt that in the concept of emptiness, the Grand Master may have been offering only something without value.

He finished his recording without insight and arranged himself for meditation. Sitting on the platform, he had a momentary feeling of wistfulness. It felt good to be on the mountain, but it was a little lonely too. He sometimes wished that his relationships with the masters were less formal, that he could be playful, or just joke with them. Saihung smiled. Such things were not permitted. But this was what he had come back for, no matter what the hardship.

He sat. This was physical stillness. He arranged his body. Cross-legged. Hands atop his knees. He became a mountain.

Regulating his breathing, Saihung made it deep. Slow. It flowed like the dense air in Huashan's caves. His blood moved as darkly and mysteriously as Huashan's underground rivers. He saw all this. He was looking within.

Meditation was a comfort. A welcome state. It was like going back to a wonderful home. It was odd. Full of contradictions. Paradoxes. By sitting still, he was getting away from those things that blocked him. By looking within, he could escape the "little self"—the everyday personality that struggled with daily problems. He put aside the Saihung that chased fascinations, experienced regret and suffering. Meditation was beautiful. Wonderful. Sublime. A living prayer. Praying and being the listener to the prayer at the same time. The most reverent feeling felt in a temple, condensed into a glowing light within. Flying and being rock still. Looking beyond what the eyes saw. Happiness and joy shared alone. A pleasure, a pain, a success, a disappointment—an understanding of how puzzle pieces fit.

Meditation was love and compassion, not like the emotion felt for lovers or children, but a feeling unmarred by selfishness. Meditation was not sensual desire. Meditation was the direct perception of the essential nature of life. While there were gods reverently sculpted in the halls, scriptures that could be chanted, robes to be worn, those were the trappings of religion. Meditation was spiritually untouched by others.

He did not need priestly robes. Nakedness was the spiritual robe.

He did not need scriptures to chant. Silence was the universal sound.

He did not need altars. His body was the altar. The gods were within him.

Meditation was an act of self-creation. He had long practiced the visualizations that shaped the mind. He could feel his meridians filling with breath, the breath formed from the compounding of his own essence with the life-giving breath of the universe. What he envisioned would affect his personality. He imagined bright light flowing along the pathways of his body, concentrating in places along his spinal cord. The image was a way of directing the mind. The power was real.

The mind abided in the body, but it wasn't just a brain. It surpassed chemistry, biology, and physics. It had to be explored and understood. Potentially infinite, it had to be comprehended. Every aspect of the mind was to be made transparent, including its drives, habits, intellect, and powers. Once that was achieved, these rare aspects of the mind were to be pared away until nothing of the self remained.

He had sometimes considered whether it was necessary to engage in so much mental effort to achieve simplicity. But the stupid could not meditate. The ignorant remained only that. Unable or unwilling to explore the mind, they were plagued by uncertainty and doubt. Insecurity was not simplicity. The ignorant remained unenlightened because they could never understand the mysteries that arose from the darkness of their own being.

As he felt the subtle strength of his internal energy, he had a sense of opening, of blooming. He always recognized the deepening consciousness, but he was often at a loss to explain or record these sensations and states of mind afterwards. They were not describable in everyday language. Maybe language was just inadequate, or maybe even holy men were not above exaggeration as they tried to capture the sense of awe and reverence with gloriously paradoxical terms. What was at once perfection and beauty to them seemed like magic to the uninitiated, and in the confusion, meditation was frequently portrayed as something supernatural. But as valuable as meditation was to Saihung, he did not find it as awesome as traditional accounts. It seemed to be utterly ordinary. It was not dramatic, but it was undeniable in its power, and it left him without a doubt that the states of mind that he experienced were true.

He was tempted to base his whole idea of existence on those states. There was an unassailable sense of his own being, something that could easily have reinforced his sense of self. His master had reminded him that he was to go further in his explorations, to pierce through his strong feelings and find on the other side of them only void. Meditation was truth; but ultimately it transcended even the highest truth so that he could emerge naked in emptiness, realize his delusion of separateness, and understand the illusory nature of existence.

In deep silence, he let his master's words return to him. In profound quiet, the solitude that existed nowhere in the whole world save his heart, he heard his master's injunction: Meditate on the transitory. He was to investigate, with the mind he had so proudly proclaimed, the fact that nothing in life lasted.

Obeying this dictum and following a memorized procedure, Saihung first examined his relationship with others to understand how everything was temporary. This was one way that he could pare away attachment that bound each person to worldly things and avoid establishing his life meaning in ties to other people. This was not easy for him. He was sentimental.

He thought of his grandparents, whom he idolized. An image of his grandmother came to him. At six feet in height, she was a ruthless woman warrior. She carried a variety of weapons with her, for the family was constantly at war both with bandits and rival warrior clans. Her favorite of the many whips she carried was made of twenty-three feet of steel link and the braided hair of her enemies. Another favorite weapon was a pair of butterfly-shaped blades with long silk tassels. Her martial arts name was "Buddhist Butterfly," though she was dainty only in appearance and name. When Saihung had scoffed at her feminine tassels, she had torn through his vest and gown with one stroke, leaving a red welt on his body. She had not even used the blade, nor her full strength. In spite of his years of training, his grandmother was one fighter Saihung never dared to challenge.

Saihung once saw his grandparents fight assassins from the neighboring Wu clan. Disguised as birthday well-wishers, the assassins approached the patriarch in the courtyard. Saihung's grandmother was sitting in a pavilion, playing the harp. As soon as she saw the flash of a dagger, she pinned the hand of the assailant with a dart that she wore as a hairpin. Her husband immediately struck with a palm blow so violent that it shattered the man's jaw.

Another drew two sabres, but the elder easily disarmed and killed him. The last two fled, running quickly through the garden gate. Saihung's grandfather sat back down with his guests. He was magnanimous, and it was his birthday. He saw no reason to slay them.

"No!" his wife cried. "One must cut the weeds and pull the roots!" With that she leapt after them and attacked with the fearsome butterfly blades.

He was of his grandparents' blood, he sprang from their lives. But they were gone, lost to the shifting of circumstances that even they in their heroic might had been unable to resist. By contemplating their temporalness, absorbing the significance of their passing, adjusting his orientation until there was no sentimentality, he saw the tyranny of attachment and delusion. Nothing in life was permanent. Nothing in life could be depended upon for one's own existence.

The Tao changed constantly. It was not fixed. There was no reason to cling to loved ones, to cherished notions, perhaps even to one's own body. Saihung shifted the focus of his meditation. He viewed his body. As much as he had shaped it into athletic supremacy, he realized it would not last. He wanted longevity, but even if he lived for eons, he knew decline was inevitable: His fingers would stiffen, his limbs would fail, the organs would dry. His body was only a temporary thing—the five elements congealed together on some fundamentally unseen level. Held together by consciousness, the uncountable fine particles would scatter once his mind let go. Whether there was heaven or hell or nothing, no one ever carried their body beyond death. It was useless to cling to it. It would not even carry him to the next world; why should he be tied to it in this one?

Saihung thought of his master, who seemed older than old, who would pass from this life. He would be but a tiny firefly changed into night. But his master held that death was but a transformation.

Death. Yes, he had seen death. He wanted only life. He wanted immortality. But as he looked at all the people gone from his life he wondered if the mind and soul were permanent. Could the mind actually transcend death and possess immortality?

If so much was a matter of the mind, if the mind itself was capable of surviving the transformations of death, was it then lasting? Could it be regarded as the ultimate truth? He first attempted to locate his own mind. It had to be within him, he reasoned. Or if it was outside, it couldn't be too far away. Was it in his brain? No, he decided. The brain was merely a physical tool of his mind. Was it the acupuncture meridians? Or the *ling qui*—the chakras? No. They too were the creations of the mind. All he saw were patterns.

Everything about his anatomy, either on the esoteric or physical level, was some pattern arranged by the mind; but the mind could not be said to be wholly within its patterns. All that he could see was the mind's manifestations. He could not see the mind itself. The mind was formless. Transparent. Opaque with mass if it wanted. Or invisible without the merest signal. Loud, as loud as a universe of sounds. Or more silent than a vacuum. But as to whether he could locate it, he did not know.

He heard his master question him again. Where was the mind?

He searched interminably. Each possibility dissolved into nothing. Was the mind on some very minute atomic level? Was it hiding in some particle? Or was it as big as the universe?

What did he know of the universe? He knew it changed. It flowed. There was no reality that could be called concrete. That was why the sages said all was illusion—not because a rock was not a rock—but because there was nowhere in the universe with a fixed point from which to base one's philosophy. There was neither anything in the body nor in the universe that was permanent enough to fix his understanding upon. He could not find his mind.

He was startled.

Did the very fact that he could not find the mind mean his master was right? Was it truly nonexistent?

The initial shock of this realization mellowed into a serenity so wonderful that he gave himself completely to it. In fact, this contemplation of his essential nonexistence was not the frightening experience he had feared. All his resistance had stemmed from simple uncertainty about the unknown. He saw a new perspective, a thrilling, wide-open possibility: All the struggles, all the ideals on which he based his life might be surrendered. Every bit of himself—created by others, and created by himself through instinct and ambition—could be allowed to float away. The mind that so furiously held his body and soul into a dense conglomeration called Kwan Saihung could simply relax, and everything he was—from physicality to imagination—would explode like a nova.

He vacillated on the cusp of this understanding. There was still a glimmer of mind, a faint breath of a human being left to contemplate its inherent nonreality. So many times his masters had told him, "The world is an illusion." Not wanting to unbalance him, they had waited this long to let him now realize, "*I* am an illusion."

"I" was made up. "I" was a by-product of the binding together of consciousness and matter. "I" was the microscopic fragment of some cosmic thought that itself was a fluke, a random occurrence, a mere ripple among an infinite number of never-conceivable universes.

All that was the self was a deception, a fairy tale to protect the fragile idea that he was a man. That he was an individual. That he was any different from rain, or stone, or stars, or dirt, or empty night. Within him was the possibility of pulling at the few threads supporting his claptrap life and letting it unravel.

A mischievous thought arose in him. It would be so easy to let go and dissolve into the void. But as much as he tried, he could not. His understanding was incomplete. There was a self to contemplate. He was still meditating. He was still a man, a monk, a martial artist, a wanderer. These identities were his anchors. They kept him grounded in life even as his excitement to explore the world gave him movement. He wasn't done with his life. Like the nearly invisible fibers connecting two halves of severed lotus root, all that he was tugged at him. The void was his to view and his to touch. But he was not yet eligible to dissolve himself in it.

THREE

The Hairpin

Meditation could not be everything. Even holy tasks could be boring and counterproductive when done to extremes. Balance was a crucial Taoist belief, and the monks rejected any fanatical activity as a violation of an all-important equilibrium. The balance to the effort of contemplative inquiry was physical work.

Working in the temples was not like working in the ordinary world. There was no exploitation of human labor and natural resources for profit. Instead, work encouraged reverence in the aspirant, even as it provided necessary support for the community. From abbot to novitiate, everyone was expected to contribute their efforts. Humility and compassion were thus affirmed. Though Taoism may well have been the ultimate doctrine of nonconformity, the residents of Huashan still found personal responsibility necessary. The monks grew their own food, repaired their own buildings, made most of their everyday articles, including furniture and clothing. Being in a temple meant being self-sufficient, grounded, and practical.

When the weather grew warmer, Saihung was assigned two responsibilities: gardening and fish farming. He was glad to have these duties, because he loved to tend living things. Watching them grow was one of his delights.

He went out in the early morning after his devotions and meditations to dig in the rich earth, to pull the weeds.

Saihung checked the greenhouses that sheltered and warmed spouting shoots. He transplanted some of the seedlings into precise rows and watered them tenderly.

Small fields for more mature vegetables were in sheltered places to protect them from the harsh winds. The Taoists had placed these gardens wherever there was sufficient light through the gorges and clefts of the mountain. Through sheer determination and hard work, they cultivated the meager fields, nurturing crops to feed the many monks.

Saihung had brought the most important farming tool with him: a flute. He had found that the plants loved music, as his masters had told him. So in addition to staking them, watering them, and pruning them, he played magnificent concerts to encourage growth. He did not care that it seemed crazy: it worked, and it was in keeping with the Taoist attitude of being one with nature.

Gardening was the Tao. It taught foresight, acceptance of change, cooperation with nature. So often he learned how a bad harvest came from a poor planting. How an insignificant defect sprang into a plant and became almost impossible to uproot. But equally true, careful and regular tending brought forth rewarding growth.

After working for several hours with the plants, Saihung next went to check on the fish. In naturally skylit grottos, the Taoists had built wooden troughs to hold carp and pike in various stages of growth from fingerlings to adult fish. He found that ice had glassed over the surface as so often happened during the cold mornings. Saihung broke away the crystal layer and scoured the troughs to remove dirt and algae, and adjusted the inflow of water through the system of bamboo pipes. He checked to see that water was still flowing freely at the inlet of the pipes.

Returning to the troughs, he fed the fish a combination of insects, grain, and chopped fungus.

Saihung wiped the sweat from his forehead and cleaned his hands. The fish also loved the flute. As he began, they gradually began to swim in the same direction. Soon they almost appeared to be dancing to his song, some thrusting their heads above the water before diving deep to the bottom of the trough. For half an hour, both Saihung and the fish gave themselves over to the music.

He heard a loud cawing. Animals often came to attack the fish, and guards were usually posted to chase them away. Today, large mountain crows were coming for their dinner. In a panic, Saihung drew grass mats over some of the troughs, but the brazen birds continued to attack. He swung his flute at some of them, but they dodged with expert swiftness.

He remembered the weapon that he had brought just for this problem and drew out a slingshot. There were too many birds flying in dizzying patterns for him to keep chasing them. He stationed himself in the center of the grotto and began firing off hard beans. There was a loud outraged squawk each time he hit a crow. The thwarted birds quickly turned toward him.

Saihung grabbed a broom to defend himself. Each time one of the furious crows closed in on him, he countered by poking the bristles at it. Soon he was dancing madly about the fish troughs, jousting with birds, until the next monk came to tend the fish. Saihung looked sheepishly at him, but the fellow only smiled and showed an even bigger broom.

As Saihung trudged back up the trail toward the temple, he reflected on the machines that had slowly begun to appear on farms. He recalled his own essays on collectivization and mechanization of agriculture, which he had written as a government official. But the monks couldn't afford machines, even if they had favored their use. For them, the measure of work was still the labor of people.

Work was a potential time of spiritual growth. They were working with nature, not against it. They were taking and giving from the earth, not shamelessly exploiting it. The harvest that they worked for was not simply for a crop of fish or vegetables, but a harvest of the Tao. When Saihung plunged his hands into the damp earth, he held the Tao. When he touched flowing water, he touched the Tao. By following the seasons, he followed the Tao. Any moment might have brought enlightenment. Realization did not come from a prayer rug, an altar, nor even from holy scripture. It was a part of life, a gift of life, and to consider realization as something separate was a fallacy. One carried the muck of fish ponds as much as one carried devotion to the gods.

In the purity of the mountain air, in the honesty of hard work and the serenity of meditation, Saihung found a refuge in which to cleanse himself of worldly things. Perhaps this time his restlessness would not return and he could spend his days in contemplation and the devotions that he now joined the other monks in performing.

He went into the temple of the Three Pure Ones, a large hall with peaked roof and pillars carved with dragons. Putting on clean robes, he washed himself at a stone basin. The cold water numbed his fingers, but he was too intent on his holy duty to care. His ablution complete, Saihung went into the darkened interior. Without greeting anyone or engaging in conversation, he stood in a row with dozens of other monks. Sandalwood incense drifted languidly through the room, candles punctuated the blackness with dim glows that reflected on gilded carvings. Behind embroidered silk curtains, in shrines that amounted to small buildings within the temple, sat the life-sized figures of Taoism's highest gods: the Original Being, the Jade Emperor, and Lao Tzu. They had been shaped by human hands, but the results had been inspired. Subtilely painted, with eyes of colored glass, dressed in real clothes, embellished with real hair, the gods seemed alive. Saihung still thought of his childhood days, when he had been afraid to enter the temples: These deities seemed alive, might have spoken to him, or moved, or punished his sins. He remembered these feelings because there was still some of that primal awe in him.

He chanted. Mist Through a Grove, dressed in bright silken colors, sang the major lines, while Saihung and the chorus took up the refrain. Their worship was almost operatic, with the use of bells, chimes, drums, and cymbals. Recitation brought the gods down to earth, balanced the powers, and above all brought humanity into balance with all natural and divine forces. Without the devotion of the human heart, the Taoists contended, there would be no balance for evil or simple entropy.

Saihung sang unreservedly. Reverence and devotion were crucial expressions to him. Through the form of scriptures, through the ceremony of standing in a consecrated building, he was bringing forth the best that he had to offer. What he gave was not the highest talent that he had, nor glibness of speech, but the simple and honest essence of his soul.

The ceremony lasted for nearly two hours. At its conclusion, Saihung went before the altar. He knelt and bowed, stood up, and knelt again. Nine times he prostrated himself before the deities. Then he slowly backed away and turned to leave the temple.

Outside, he felt the frigid evening air approaching. He looked into the blackening sky, shimmering crimson at the horizon, deepening to black at its highest vault. He could already see a star, and the moon was already visible. It seemed to lead a current of icy cold down through the peaks and canyons. He shivered. It would be time for padded clothes again.

Autumn would be coming soon. The maples had already turned red, and the higher parts of the mountain had already seen some snow flurries. He saw the orange reflections of new snow on the mountains surrounding Huashan. He knew that he would have to prepare soon. Once snow set in, descending the mountain was impossible. Any slip on the ice might send him plunging thousands of feet.

He went to the kitchen of the main temple. This large, cluttered room with hanging herbs and pots was nearly the only warm place around. Cooks rushed to prepare the evening meal, their long hair wrapped in cloth. Some were stationed at enormous pots, standing on the brick stoves to stir vegetable stews. Others quickly fried gluten and more vegetables. A few tended to the ovens, for bread, not rice, was the staple in the area. Young novices fed the wood-burning fires.

Saihung carried a bowl of noodles and vegetables in one hand, a lantern in the other. It was a holy day, so the priests could not have any fish. Sometimes it seemed to the constantly hungry Saihung that there were all too many such festivals. He wanted to return to his hut and eat alone that night. By absorbing the quietness, he hoped to renew his efforts. Nearly every day he thought that he had the answer to satisfy his master, and each time he was rewarded with gentle chiding or a rebuke.

The room was bitterly cold. He lit an oil lamp and piled wood into the bronze brazier. As he was about to eat his meal, he was startled to see his master at the door.

Saihung rushed to kneel. The Grand Master stepped lightly into the room. He was immaculate in his black robes.

The Grand Master stood for a while without saying anything. Saihung was reminded of the first time he had looked into the old man's eyes. There was something mysterious and hypnotically attractive about them. For long moments, Saihung felt as if there was no other presence in the world for him. He regretted that his own grandfather was dead. He wished that his master was more like a grandfather, that there was more warmth and intimacy to their relationship. But in the temple, the roles of master and student were severely defined.

He was unaware how absorbed he had become until the Grand Master ended the long silence with an announcement.

"Your destiny is incomplete," declared his master. "You must not seek it here in China, but across the oceans."

Saihung was surprised at the abruptness of his master's pronouncement.

"Master, all I want is to serve you," he said.

"You cannot, yet. You must fulfill your quest."

"Then I'll do it and come quickly back," replied Saihung immediately.

"No. Don't come back."

Saihung was silent.

"I may not be here when you come back," added his master.

"What are you saying? Why won't you be here?"

"Don't question! Go out to fulfill your quest."

"But master! What is my task?" There was a tone of desperation in his voice.

"That is for you to find out," said his master firmly. "I know both the question and the answer. Do not return until you can tell me." The Grand Master turned and left.

A few moments passed before Saihung realized that he was sitting with his mouth agape. A burst of anger came up in him. He seized his bowl and flung it against the wall. He jumped up, staring angrily about, cornered. Saihung pulled the silver hairpin that pegged his hair and brought it before him. This was the Grand Master's gift when he had ordained Saihung over two decades before. Saihung punched the window open and threw the hairpin off the mountainside.

Chinese of Pittsburgh

Saihung stood with a friend on the Sixth Street Bridge. The Allegheny River was below him, midnight reflections undulating on its inky surface. Central Pittsburgh, Pennsylvania, a dense pile of decaying brick buildings, was behind him. Cars rumbled steadily over the humpback span, shaking the girders and dirtying the snow that had fallen only recently. Saihung steadied himself against the stinging wind and gripped the twine handles of his shopping bag. Even with gloves on, the heavy groceries seemed to cut into his palm. His friend, Sam Lee, offered to help, but Saihung refused. This was the first time they had walked home together after work.

Sam was a slender man in his twenties. His Chinese name, Lee San, actually meant that he was the third child in his family, and the community had simply transliterated his name to an English one. He pulled a scarf more tightly around his neck. "Have you been in the United States long?" he asked.

"About two years," replied Saihung.

"Then you should have much experience with this country."

Saihung thought a moment. "No, I have never quite become used to this nation. The people are not always easy to understand. Some treat you well once you get to know them, but most can be mean. Everything is so different here." He wanted to add that he still felt frightened and lonely.

"Yes," agreed Sam. "It is a struggle to be here. This is not an easy life. One has to go where one can to make a living. I was just a farmer in the hills. If my uncle had not sponsored me, I might still be scrounging for a living in the villages."

Saihung had long ago made the decision to keep his past a secret. "Yes, me too. My uncle and aunt, the Yees, sponsored me here. Now I not only have to work to survive, but to repay and support them as well. They are getting old and have no one to help them."

"A Yee?" asked Sam with a rueful smile. "We're not supposed to be friends."

"My uncle and aunt aren't blood relatives," replied Saihung. "But I know that the Lees and Yees are sworn enemies."

"Oh, who knows why they fight?" said Sam. "I know only that my grandfather hated the Yees. No one actually remembers what the feud is about."

"This is America," said Saihung. "What difference does it make now?"

"Yes, that feud is a part of home," said Sam as he gazed across the river. "And home is very far away."

They stopped for a moment at the highest arch of the yellow-green suspension bridge. Lee was considerate enough to let Saihung pause in as much solitude as was available on a nighttime highway. He was good company, Saihung thought as they walked toward the North Shore where they both lived. Both had longing memories of home and hopes that were ill-defined dreams.

As he stood stoically over the water, he wanted to cry out, to lament in terrible tones to his heaven that was gone. Instead of living in his paradise, he was now an outcast. He felt hapless, wretched. He was condemned to wander in search of some unnamed destiny. His master had condemned him to walk the paths of exile, deprived of glory, bereft of blessings, stripped of joy.

He let out a silent sigh that registered as a cloud of breath before him. He had been exiled from Huashan for two years with no further explanation or instructions. Hoping for guidance, he thought back to the first time that he had met the Grand Master.

"His spirit did not need to return to this dusty world," the Grand Master had said when Saihung's potential discipleship had been broached by his grandfather. "He came willingly. But those who volunteer to return are given a task. If he is to fulfill his mission, he will need long training." But his education had apparently not provided a way to determine what his mission was, nor did it equip him to deal with living in America. At one time, his master had told him to help all those on his path who were suffering. Surely, he reasoned, that couldn't be the task. Even if it was, that was impossible to achieve as a waiter struggling to survive.

"Are you thinking of General Yang?" asked Lee softly.

Saihung turned to look at him. Lee's thin and crooked face was made alternately pale and black by the passing headlights. He was talking about a cook who worked with them. General Yang had introduced Saihung and Lee, dishwasher, to one another.

"No," replied Saihung honestly. "I have always loved bridges. I like to look over them at the water. It always seems so peaceful."

"Ah, back home, the bridges are like that," agreed Lee. "Like the moon bridges, so perfectly round. I also liked to walk over them, especially when I was a boy. They told me that ghosts could not cross water. I liked that. It's a lie, though, isn't it?"

"Why talk this way?"

Lee looked at him with an expression at once terrible and sympathetic.

"Didn't you hear at work? General Yang killed himself last night. He jumped from this bridge—split his head on the river bottom."

Saihung was stunned. He looked out at the rippling water. A dredging barge slid beneath them. The bridge was not that high. He wanted to say "No!" to the news, but he had learned to accept death silently, no matter how suffocating that was.

"It's hard to believe," said Saihung, gazing toward the point where the Allegheny joined the Ohio River. "One day a man is here, the next day he is gone. It's like a dream." He thought of Yang's military bearing, his pacing up and down the kitchen as if he was still commanding the battlefield. "He lost too much," Saihung mused. "He lost his faith in a Nationalist China, lost his rank, lost his wife. He loved only gambling and his son. Once he said to me, 'Every man has his motivation, the thing he must do. Family is what is important to me. The state will abandon you, fortune will abandon you. Only family is worth struggling for.'"

"He died because of his son," said Lee quietly when Saihung finished his recollections. Saihung had seen a photo of the twenty-year-old, bespectacled youth. The picture had been like a votive object, the general's wallet like a tabernacle.

"How could that be?"

"The son caught tuberculosis. He needed medical attention."

"All Yang wanted was to be reunited with his son. He was saving for years."

"It wasn't enough for the expenses."

"He should have come to me."

"As if you're rich?" asked Lee sadly. "No, he had to raise more money than any of us have. He was also too proud to ask for help."

"So what did he do?" asked Saihung.

"Gambled," said Lee bluntly.

"Oh, no." Saihung could see it coming.

"Yes," Lee continued. "He gambled all last night. He lost nearly all. He risked everything on the last gambit. He lost that too. Yang was so desperate that he even asked the dealers for a loan, some help. But you know how merciless gamblers are. They found him this morning. The family associations are going to take care of the funeral."

"It's a little late, isn't it?" said Saihung bitterly. "That money could have gone to save two men."

"They don't think that way," shrugged Sam as they started walking again.

They walked through a railroad underpass and crossed Sandusky street at the corner of East Ohio. There was a soldier's monument on the corner. At the foot of the weathered marble were dozens of flowers—many artificial—and a brown, somewhat tattered American flag. It was what might have passed for a roadside shrine in China, a place where he might have prayed. But there was no place here to pray for a man's soul.

He looked down East Ohio Street, the shopping thoroughfare for the neighborhood. It was a darkened corridor of brick buildings, mostly built in the late 1880s. They were cramped Victorian gothics, sagging, holding each other up, sheltering dim and shabby storefronts, snow and shadow pooling deeply in the windows and doors. Most had ornate Romanesque decorations that had long ago lost their charm to the erosion of ice and time.

Saihung was still brooding about Yang when they came to Sandusky Park, a large tree-scattered field about two blocks in area. On sunny days, he had sat there with Yang. Though the park was nothing but bench, lawn, and tree, the two had tried to imagine a tranquility beyond the roaring traffic.

The park was the interceding zone between the downtown area and their neighborhood. It was fastest to walk through the park. Saihung had never thought much of it. But Sam was suddenly nervous.

"Kwan, I did not tell you something," he told Saihung in a trembling voice.

"What do you mean?"

"Every night I am chased through this park. They beat me. I run all the way home, bar myself inside. They have painted my windows with tar, threatened to attack my wife."

"Calm down," said Saihung. "I see no one. Perhaps they won't come with two people."

"I hope so," said Lee dubiously. He anxiously lit a cigarette.

Tall leafless trees made the area gloomy. Cars drove by, but the traffic was not reassuring. Clearly, no one would get out of their cars to help if trouble came; perhaps they wouldn't even notice. The autos circled all four sides of the park. They were anonymous steel shells.

As Lee feared, three men awaited them. Saihung scanned their bodies by reflex. There was one large fat one, with greasy hair. The one standing in the middle was tall, heavily muscled across the chest and shoulders. The third was more lanky, but had the cruelest face. Saihung noted their characteristics with satisfaction. The key to his way of fighting was to ascertain all his opponents' weaknesses before words were spoken or blows exchanged.

"Hey, Chink! Brought a friend?" asked the tall one with a sardonic tilt of his head.

Saihung was quiet. He knew there was no way that Lee could understand what was being said to him. But threatening countenances were perhaps more traumatic than words.

"What's the matter, Chink? Cat got your tongue?" said the fat one.

"He doesn't understand you, stupid," returned the tall one. "Try ching-ching-chong-ding-dong!"

They laughed.

"Come here, Chinaman!" said the tall man, grabbing Lee by the shirt.

"Stop!" ordered Saihung, putting down his shopping bag.

"Shut up, asshole! We'll get you later."

Saihung liked to get close to someone when he fought. "I didn't hear," said Saihung, stepping right up to the man.

"Jesus Christ!" exclaimed the tall one. "This shithead doesn't know how to mind his own business!"

He let go of Lee and reached out to grab Saihung. Bringing his hand up to intercept, Saihung laid his wrist on top of his opponent's arm. One touch was all a good fighter needed to assess the strength of his adversary.

"Pretty bold, aren't you?" shouted the man.

Saihung said nothing. He only looked steadily back. His eyes did not blink, but his face changed. A look of hunger and eagerness came over him. He was like a predator looking at a tiny victim.

"Hey, dumb shit," continued the man threateningly, "I'm going to wipe that stupid look right off your face."

"I don't think so," replied Saihung as his eyes opened in anticipation.

The instant that he felt movement, Saihung's forward hand struck the tall man's abdomen with a blow so violent that it doubled him over. Saihung followed with a rapid blow to the neck. The muscular man staggered forward, gasping for air.

The others came at him, but Saihung used the first as a shield. Dazed, the cruel man was easily maneuvered. Saihung did not drop him until he had taken a good many fists and sticks from his companions.

Saihung dispatched the fat one with a rapid knee to the bladder followed by a blow to the heart. A thrill, a power surged through Saihung. There was a unique release for him when he fought. He stepped head-on as the hard-faced one charged again. Saihung blocked his blow, hit him hard in the ribs. He followed by stepping behind him, and brought an elbow down. A satisfying thud smashed his opponent to the ground, but the man got up immediately.

"I'm going to kill you!" he cried.

Saihung stepped back. "Listen. I let you get up. That's a first for me. If you come again, I'm putting you in the hospital!"

"You full-of-shit-motherfucker!"

He tried to ram Saihung with a head-butt. Saihung sidestepped and brought a forearm into the midsection. Elbow around the neck, Saihung threw him again onto the ice-layered cement. A kick brought the snap of cracking ribs.

The tall one grabbed a stick and brought it through the air. Saihung whirled around. He blocked the arm while it was still up and brought his knee up, stooping the man over. Two quick combinations brought a spray of teeth and blood.

He fell on Saihung, panting and heaving. By reflex, Saihung would normally have struck him ten more times before his assailant hit the pavement. Instead, he caught him involuntarily.

So adept at improvising movement, so sharp were his abilities, that his touch instantly registered numerous options for further mauling the man. He paused. The jaw, against his bicep, was slack. Blood and spit blotted through his sleeve. The head felt surprisingly heavy. If it had been China of ten years before, he would have removed this man from the world like an imperfect vase. Here was a man. His to kill.

He had fought since his youth, even though he knew that killing brought retribution against one's soul. For the sake of women, children, and his homeland, he had gladly volunteered for war, willing to accept that consequence. As for martial duels, he and his opponents both acknowledged death as an integral part of the arrangement. There was a certain nobility and honor to his fighting. But here, there were only racist bigots, idiots. He disdained them. There was no glory in killing them. Saihung threw the man down and found the shaken and pallid Lee.

"We won't mention this, will we?" said Saihung.

"No! No!" agreed Lee hoarsely. "I hope this ends it. I had no idea you could fight."

"Forget it," said Saihung. "A little exercise before bed is healthy."

Saihung saw Lee to the door of his home before walking the three more blocks to his home. Though the fever to fight had worn off, he still thought about his confrontation. There was nothing heroic or principled about this type of fighting. He had not changed anyone's mind, had not remedied anything. It had simply been a primitive assertion of will. But worse than regret for the battle, he disliked being forced to consider issues never mentioned in scripture, sermon, nor even in politics. Frankly, he had

had few decisions to make on Huashan, and he liked that. The masters made all the decisions. They knew what was right and wrong. But since he had left China, he had had to make all his own decisions and make judgments with no precedence in his life.

Saihung returned to the park the next day, on his way to Chinatown for supplies. There was no sign of his nocturnal struggle. He watched a few mothers escorting warmly dressed children to the park's community center, and then went directly to the bridge. Walking southward through the main business district, he came to the settlement situated on the north and south sides of a small rectangular block. A few buildings faced onto Third Street, dwarfed by the height of the imposing Grant Building, and a few more faced south on the next street over, their view of the Monongahela River obscured by the wedge of a highway on-ramp.

The one single building identifiable as "Chinese" was the headquarters for the Peaceful Harmony Labor Organization, a three-story brownstone with fake tile roofs and wooden balconies that echoed the buildings of Canton. A Chinese restaurant on the ground floor proclaimed itself to be "Chinatown Inn." Beneath it was the single word "Cuisine."

A few doors down was Big Mrs. Lee's store, New Horizons. It was a four-story nineteenth-century brick building that had housing for old, unmarried men. New Horizons was the only place to go if he wanted to buy tofu, dried goods, herbs, or preserves from China. Mrs. Lee imported Chinese vegetables from New York. These were usually frozen or wilted, but they still satisfied the craving for familiar flavors. They were displayed in the crates that they had arrived in, propped open in front of the store.

Saihung took two brown paper bags off an iron rack and began to pick some snow peas and cabbage.

At the front of the store was the cash register. Mr. Lee, a slender, bespectacled man with graying hair, was stationed there. He was slow moving, his mind always on some abstract thought. He had been a scholar, and still loved to discuss the classics with the men, or his children with the women. He boasted endlessly about his son the doctor, his favorite married daughter, how well the younger ones were doing in school. He still retained the romantic notion that business was an improper activity for an academic man. Accordingly, he could neither add nor subtract adequately. The shrewd Mrs. Lee rushed to wait on Saihung as soon as he entered the store. She was terrified that her husband would err at the cash register, as always, in favor of the customer.

Mrs. Lee was the unquestioned queen of Chinatown. She was fat, fair-skinned, a woman with a golden smile. By design or poor health, every tooth in her mouth was pure gold, accentuated by crimson lipstick. Her hair was perfectly coiffed in a permanent wave. Her friends would come to pay homage to her every week, and comment on her good health. She would only reply with uncharacteristic self-deprecation that she was overweight. They would always say it was because she was blessed with fortune and happiness. Mrs. Lee was landlady, proprietor, mother, helpful savior, and of course, town gossip.

There were no oracles in Pittsburgh, but near or far, she seemed to know everything as it happened. Marriages, births, affairs, deaths, hidden secrets were all parts of her oral history. She talked constantly with the old women who sat in rosewood chairs at the side of the store. In winter, they warmed themselves by a wood stove. In summer, they languidly cooled themselves with eagle-feather fans. Their discussions formed a constant commentary on community events.

As he shopped, Saihung could hear Big Mrs. Lee and her chorus gossip about the laundryman Yu, who had been exiled from China for raping his own mother; the old scholar Wu, who slept only in a chair with his arms closed vampire-style; the recent government raid on the opium den on Sandusky Street; the many Chinese youngsters who were running off with Western girls, and getting married because they had to.

"Did you hear about the poor boy drowned by his white university classmates?" Saihung heard one woman ask another.

"Yes, that was Fifth Lee's son," replied another. "It's a tragedy! He received scholarships to engineering school. They were obviously jealous."

Big Mrs. Lee stopped weighing Saihung's vegetables.

"Shouldn't someone go to the police?"

"They won't take the word of Chinese over whites," said Saihung.

"That's true, Ox Boy," said Mrs. Lee, using the nickname the community had given the muscular Saihung. "Still, it's terrible. He had so much promise. The companies would have hired him right out of school. Imagine! A Lee! A professional!"

"But dead," said one of the old women bluntly. "Stupid kid! He was so excited when they invited him to a picnic. What a fool to go boating with them when he knew that he could not swim."

Mrs. Lee returned to Saihung's vegetables. "Tragic! Tragic!"

She bagged all of Saihung's purchases and looked at him.

"Don't you be so trusting," she told him.

"I'm not that way," replied Saihung.

"Oh yes, we've all heard about you," smiled Mrs. Lee.

"What do you mean?"

"We all know how you defended Sam the dishwasher," said Mrs. Lee admiringly.

"Please don't mention it," said Saihung, blushing.

"You're too modest!" she exclaimed, slapping his arm insinuatingly. Saihung retreated in embarrassment. It was one thing to knock men to the ground. It was another to face the talkative Mrs. Lee.

Saihung left the store cursing Lee the dishwasher. Everyone thought that martial artists were heroes. Children wanted to emulate them, older people looked upon them as knights for a cause. But he himself knew that being a martial artist was no easy matter. He had sustained many injuries over the years, blows that had distorted his body, struggles that had tired him to the soul. He had paid a high price to reach the point where a brawl in the park was an easy matter.

He walked back toward the Sixth Street Bridge. The afternoon was graying toward a chilly evening. The air was thick with dust, coal, smoke, car exhaust, and oddly enough, the smell of catsup; the Heinz 57 factory was on the North Shore. Snow was bright on the railings, dirty on the ground. The street lamps, rusted stalks, had not been lit.

He stopped in the twilight to read the bronze plaque on the courthouse that was inscribed with the Pledge of Allegiance. The Constitution, Declaration of Independence, Pledge of Allegiance, and the history of the Revolutionary and Civil Wars had all influenced him to emigrate to the United States. He had pictured dense forests stretching to the ocean shores, distant mountains of lofty magnificence, Native Americans of all the different tribes, people dressed in colonial costume as well as the modern clothes that he had seen in movies (after all, in China, a few centuries did not affect fashion unduly, and different minority groups maintained their traditional clothing). As he thought over his fight and the drowning, the last line of the Pledge took on a new irony.

He wondered if he had made the wrong decision to come to the United States. He was in a huge, grim city dominated by the sound and smoke of steel mills, walking on paved streets beside cars, living in squat, geometric buildings that had arteries of galvanized plumbing and nerves of electric wire. There was no place in the city for jade, silk gowns, books written on delicate mulberry paper, fans with calligraphy, proud horses, or flutes of purple bamboo. All that he had of himself was in his heart, or locked in a chest at home, or to be shared with a few acquaintances.

Saihung walked down East Ohio Street to a black-painted entrance of Romanesque columns and an archway, and climbed the stairs to a small second-floor room. There were a few vinyl booths and a diner-style counter with stools. The chrome edges and stool supports were tarnished, the upholstery repaired here and there with plastic tape. The ancient clock had a yellow film over it, and its tail of electric cord was twisted and cracking. As usual, there were no customers.

A short man in his fifties greeted him. Lithe and flexible would never describe Uncle Feng; he was like a fireplug on legs. His neck was thick and stiff, and it supported a balding head with a face interested purely in expediency. He was dressed in white cook's clothes with short sleeves that showed heavy forearms and rough, thick-fingered hands, abundantly scarred from cuts and burns. Uncle

Feng wasn't actually his relative; it was just how a younger man addressed an older one. Saihung was glad to know some people who represented something familiar, and he could not be comfortable with the gabbing women at New Horizons. Uncle Feng had been a boxer before he had become a restaurant owner.

"Hey Ox Boy! It's cold outside!" said Uncle Feng.

"Yes it is," replied Saihung, wondering about the Chinese habit of greeting others by announcing the obvious.

"Come in, and take your coat off," said Uncle Feng as he walked back into the kitchen. Saihung could hear something sizzling in the wok.

Saihung hung his things on one of the antler-like metal coatracks and followed his host.

"Old Poon is late as usual," grumbled Feng. "He's never on time. And I have made some of the finest delicacies from our home province. Here. Help me cut some vegetables."

Saihung picked up a cleaver and stationed himself at a chopping block that was a simple cross section of a log. He quickly sliced carrots, celery, cabbage, and chard. In the meantime, Uncle Feng began cooking at a wok fired by leaping flames. His spatula beat a quick cadence on the iron. The vegetables in the pan roared like firecrackers when water hit the hot oil. Oil, wine, and soy were his main seasonings, and he produced beautiful dishes glistening with just the right amount of sauce.

Within twenty minutes, they sat down to a feast of catfish steamed with black beans, a crispy fried chicken, sauteed scallops with vegetables, braised pork, and hot steamed rice. Saihung shared everything but the pork. This always provoked a comment from Uncle Feng.

"A man who never eats pork! It's abnormal!"

Saihung only shrugged as he ate mouthful after mouthful of the fragrant and juicy food. No one knew he was a Taoist. Only he knew why he practiced certain restrictions.

Uncle Feng filled a glass with Johnny Walker. He motioned to Saihung to have a drink, though by now both knew it to be formality.

"I get tipsy," Saihung explained ineffectively.

"Youngster!" laughed Feng. "That's OK. There's just more for me and Old Poon."

There was a noise at the stairs.

"That must be the bastard now," said Feng, his face beginning to redden from the liquor.

"Did you two begin eating without me?" bellowed a voice from the door.

"You never eat with us anyway!" retorted Feng with the voice of an insulted cook.

"Huh! It's just that I have my preferences." There was the noise of a bicycle kickstand.

"Don't mar the walls!"

"Relax before you have a heart attack!"

Uncle Poon came charging up the stairs. Though he was nearly sixty-five and white-haired, he was straight-backed and vital. He made his living as a mover. Heavyset, he had large hands that he usually kept at his side as if at attention. He had been a seaman most of his life, and his expertise with knots made him one of the most sought after men among the Chinese of Pittsburgh. Whenever anyone sent a box or trunk to China, it was Uncle Poon who bound it with manila rope. Saihung had seen him carry a steamer trunk on his back, and there was almost nothing he couldn't move with ropes, levers, or most frequently, his own brawn.

Uncle Poon was poor and usually wore the same clothes. His pants were held up by a length of rope and he wore the same wool coat in summer or winter. It was long, with the eccentric tailoring of many odd pockets sewn to the interior. These pockets might hold a slip of paper, a bit of twine, sometimes even a coin, but they were usually empty.

He came to the table and pulled his coat back to display his muscular girth. His head was as massive as an elephant skull, his skin brown, tight, and shiny. Incongruously, he had a tiny mouth and delicate wire-rimmed glasses balanced crookedly around his wide face.

"So why are you late?" mumbled Feng.

"I was held up," said Poon in English.

"Held up doing what?" asked Saihung.

"No, not held up, busy. I mean *held up*."

"You mean you were robbed?" asked Saihung with concern.

"Yes!" roared Uncle Poon with a knowing look at Feng. "After all, I'm old and yellow-skinned. Those American boys think I'm an easy target!"

Saihung smiled. He knew Uncle Poon was a veteran of waterfront brawls. He also knew that the old man liked to talk.

"So what happened?" asked Saihung obligingly.

"He stopped me as I was getting on my bicycle. He wanted my money. He had a knife."

"Stupid kid," muttered Feng. It wasn't clear if he thought the would-be mugger dumb because Poon was poor, or because of Poon himself.

"So I stood with my arms out. That idiot went through every one of my pockets—and even *I'm* not sure how many pockets are in this thing."

Uncle Poon paused dramatically, as if to give his two friends time to mentally tabulate the possible number of his pockets.

"He was mad when he was all done. Then I smashed him!" He shot out a fist the size of an anvil. Uncle Feng began laughing with delight.

"I just made some dentist rich," Uncle Poon concluded as he walked into the kitchen.

Saihung and Uncle Feng returned to their dinner as they heard Poon light the burner. He had his own peculiarities in eating. Uncle Poon loved to eat something never gotten in China: T-Bone steak. He heated the wok until it was smoking, quickly poured oil in, and threw the big piece of meat down. He seared it quickly over high heat, turned it over, and it was done.

Uncle Poon came to the table with the sizzling hot steak, rice, and a few seared vegetables. He poured some catsup and steak sauce and immediately attacked with knife and fork. Hot blood ran over his plate, staining the rice red. The steak was not rare. It was warm and raw.

"Barbarian!" said Feng disgustedly.

"Just pour the whisky, you old miser!"

Feng did so, taking the opportunity to fill his own glass again.

"I'll have to catch up," commented Uncle Poon.

"Don't worry," replied Uncle Feng. "You can drink Ox Boy's share."

Poon quickly devoured the steak with great pleasure. "Ahh, except for steak, I wish I was back in Foshan," said Uncle Poon.

"Oh, the food in Foshan, Ox Boy. You've never tasted anything like it!" agreed Uncle Feng.

Saihung thought back over the many banquets and feasts he had tasted in rooms of sandalwood. Yes, Cantonese food was delicious, he acknowledged. Hadn't Emperor Qianlong disguised himself just to travel and taste southern cooking?

"Yes!" said Uncle Poon enthusiastically when Saihung mentioned the emperor's name.

"That emperor was smart. And he was a good fighter too!"

"But cruel," interjected Feng. "After all he burned down Shaolin!"

They were referring to the temple where Boddhidharma had first introduced Zen Buddhism and that had become a notable center of martial arts. It had also become a virtual center of anti-Imperial rebellion in the eighteenth century, and Qianlong had attacked it to destroy the patriots. Many colorful people lived during that time, and their histories had since become folk legends. Thinking of the China of temples and poetry, where one man or one place could generate centuries of history, Saihung's mind filled with a plethora of images—the most colorful time of martial arts, of heroines such as Wu Mei the fighting nun, or heroes like the White Eyebrow Taoist Priest, achievements in porcelains, paintings reserved for the emperor's palace, and special banquet dishes reputed to have originated at that time.

Saihung immersed himself in sentiment as the old men drank. Where was the China of pageantry and beauty? Where was his master, his temple, his classmates? Where was the life he had aspired to, the life of wandering in a landscape thick with webs of historical association? In China, any given spot might hold tales both real and mythological. There might be stories of friendship, a famous duel, a spot where a god had come to earth, a place where lovers had met, a river where dragons slept.

Instead, he was a stranger in a country not even two

hundred years old, among a population that expected its achievements would last forever. Instead of different cuisines in every province, everything seemed to be the same—hot dogs, steaks, and fried chicken. Instead of deep history, there were but few wars, slavery, persecution, and genocide. Instead of quiet places tied to nature, there were mighty buildings, trains, planes, hordes of cars. He was a stranger here.

"I'm old," said Feng as he got more drunk. "But if I could, I'd go back."

"I wouldn't," announced Uncle Poon firmly. "I'd be even more poor in China."

"Would you go back, Kwan?" asked Feng.

"I don't know." How could he tell them he had a quest to fulfill? How could he say that it was an imperative from a time and a place that seemed so unreal now?

"Why don't you go back? Get married."

"Married?" smiled Saihung. "I'm not the type."

"Every man is the type!" laughed Feng.

"Well, you two are single," retorted Saihung.

"You think it's so easy in this country?" asked Feng.

"It doesn't matter," said Poon glumly. "Too old. Too poor. Too ugly. If one had even one saving quality it would be all right. For example, if you're rich, you could buy a bride no matter how old and ugly you were. But us? As they say," and here he switched to English, "three strikes and you're out!"

They all laughingly agreed.

"So did you just come to get rich, like all of us?" Feng asked Saihung.

"Well, I was traveling and heard America was a different country," replied Saihung honestly.

"Different than what?" asked Poon in a perplexed voice.

"I read the Constitution and the Declaration of Independence. I thought it would be a wonderful place."

"Stupid idealistic bookworm!" cursed Feng.

Uncle Poon drained his glass. "Well, I certainly hope you got those notions out of your head!"

"You're drunk!" warned Feng.

"I am not!" insisted Poon. "And anyway, does that invalidate what I've said?"

"Ox Boy here is sensitive and idealistic," returned Feng. "Why spoil it?"

"So he reads books," shrugged Poon. "I'm trying to give him a real education."

"Suit yourself," said Feng. "I'm going to do the dishes."

Uncle Poon turned shakily toward Saihung. He leaned over close enough for his Scotch breath to roar across the table.

"Let me tell you, young man, what a Caucasian man once told me," said Uncle Poon forcefully. " 'Ten Chinaman aren't as good as one nigger!' You know how they treat blacks. Guess the rest!"

Saihung only smiled and poured more whisky for Poon. Perhaps it was inevitable that drunken gatherings always turned ugly. He picked up his dishes and helped Feng with the dishes before he ventured into the night frost. Saihung was still young enough to dismiss Poon's remark as mere cynicism.

Saihung lived with his aunt and uncle a few blocks away from Feng's on Foreland Street, in the eastern half of a sagging wooden duplex. Two stories high, with attic and gables, it had been built after the Civil War and its yellow and green paint had never been renewed. Saihung walked up the few steps to the door and inserted his key into the nearly useless lock. Warm air flowed at him from the dark hallway. That was the nice thing about staying with retired people, he thought. They kept the house a comfortable temperature.

He hung up his outer clothing and crept down the hall as quietly as possible. His aunt and uncle had their bedroom on the first floor. There was nothing else on the main floor but a small shrine to Guan Yin, the Goddess of Mercy. The original house was one-room deep, with the kitchen in an added-on section. In fact, the rear of the house was of several different supplemental structures, all added at various occasions with no regard to the surrounding architecture.

He walked into the kitchen, no longer noticing how its floor tilted at an angle different from the hall. Thoughtfully, his aunt had left a table lamp lit in the kitchen, and Saihung headed toward the slit of yellow light showing through the partially opened door. He smiled. The couple had surely argued about the cost of electricity versus the meaning of a gesture.

The kitchen was painted yellow over often-repaired plaster. The huge, streamlined white-enameled stove and refrigerator dominated the square room. The pink and green countertops were cluttered with tins of flour, tea, and other goods. In a corner, on the green linoleum floor, sat a twenty-five-gallon glass jar filled with rice.

Saihung put some water on the stove to boil, watching the flower of blue flame bloom with a poof under the old steel kettle. He reminded himself to grab it off the burner before its indecent whistle shocked the neighborhood.

As he turned toward the formica table with its chrome legs, he noticed an envelope. There on the thin paper was his master's familiar calligraphy, along with a shaky English address written by someone else. He sat down to read it. He was careful: The kitchen chairs were some modern, zig-zag, S-shape of chrome tubing and red-vinyl-covered plywood. He was forever in danger of pitching back in the silly things.

The letter was short:

> I am leaving the mountain.
> Come back to help.

It ended with the official seal of the abbot of Huashan.

Saihung put the letter down. His master's calligraphy was as beautiful as ever, but he was not impressed by the message. His first reaction was that he would go immediately. His second thought was: Why should I? After all, he had been practically expelled from the mountain. He still felt a little hurt. They had raised him from a youth but had pushed him out when he had most wanted guidance. He had the jealous suspicion that his master's acolytes and his other classmates were all learning the secrets of immortality while he was waiting on tables in some chop suey house.

He read the letter again. It wasn't all that easy to travel to the other side of the world. It wasn't cheap; it wasn't quick; and it wouldn't necessarily be a happy reunion.

Saihung opened the back door to the garden and stepped through the black opening. The neighbor's dog began barking immediately. A soft moonlight fell on the worn wooden porch. The house seemed to hold years of melancholy. He descended the cracked and moaning steps.

The midnight cold stung him. His skin contracted involuntarily with the shock, and he could feel the blood flood his cheeks as his body made an effort to maintain his warmth. The snow beneath his feet crunched with each step. He stuck his hands into his pockets.

The garden was small, just the leftover space after the haphazard additions to the duplex. There was a lawn in the summer that was usually brown from the southern exposure; but now it was covered with a three-foot layer of frosty white. In the middle of the expanse was the skeleton of a peach tree. Saihung had planted it there when he had first moved to the city. Still barely beyond a sapling, it stood straight but lonely in the snow.

There was not a leaf on it. From the outside, he might not have even been able to tell that it was alive. It seemed dead, withered, cold. No buds showed, not even an insect crawled on the nude branches. There was no way to know whether it was going to survive the winter. Spring might come and it might still stand there just as forlorn and devoid of life. If it sprouted again, it meant that this botanical corpse had enough consciousness to have patience. There was faith that it would survive the winter, that it could even forego its life-supporting leaves in the knowledge that light and warmth would come again.

He asked himself if he should go back. Perhaps if he were back in an intact China, he would have consulted a fortune-teller or cast the yarrow stalks of the *I Ching*. But he was without such crutches. He had to do what the elders had taught him to do since childhood: read the patterns in nature. A tree stood on a spot of power. Its branches took on their formation for a reason. They reached out to the power spots in the atmosphere. Thus one could "read" a tree. It had lessons to give, even power to transmit. Its branches were calligraphy. He stood in the dim moonlight, looking at the apparently dead tree. He thought of his own desperation, his own resentment of being separated from Huashan. Somewhere in all this madness, this working in restaurants, this being attacked, this living in a foreign land, was supposed to be some answer for him. He had believed that there would be a key of reason that would illuminate all his strivings.

Saihung thought back over his fight in the park. He wondered how long it would be before he would start thinking like everyone else. Drink. Gamble. Get married. Beat up on others until someone stronger brings you down. He had been raised with the ultimate goals of education, wealth, and spirituality. That still did not guarantee that he could gently live and grow. He had been provided with philosophy and guidance, had known whisperings from divine voices. Now those were swept away by profanity and trauma. Somehow, he who should have been the most privileged, the most fortunate, the bravest, and the most skilled, was now as wretched as any other. Being raised in a monastery and taking holy vows did not guarantee that he would not be subjected to economic hardship and racism.

He reached out and touched a branch. He had started out from something small, had been but a seedling. Had his master not nurtured him and pruned him and cared for him, he would never have reached this point. His master had sent him into the world. Saihung resented it. But he remembered the old expression: The seedling does not grow tall in the shadow of a larger tree.

He went back inside without expression. The dog began to bark again. Saihung turned out the light and climbed the stairs to his room. He took a shower, washing his hair though it was but a crewcut now.

As he prepared for sleep, he looked at the letter again. Going back to China was not going to be salvation. It was going back to run an errand. Still, as much as he half-resented his master for propelling him on these wanderings, he knew he would go back to help him.

FIVE

The End of Huashan

Saihung traveled from Pittsburgh to San Francisco by train, crossed the Pacific on the American President Line's SS *President Wilson*, went quickly through Hawaii, Yokohama, Hong Kong. A boat to Guangdong, and a series of train rides first through the province of Jiangsi, then the cities of Hangzhou and Xian, took him hundreds of miles into the interior. He crossed nearly the whole of Shaanxi province by rail to reach the foot of Huashan. It was spring of 1953. Travel was slow and it wasn't easy.

He gave himself all sorts of excuses during the month-long journey. He would be seeing Huashan again. Worship at all the old places. Get away from America. Maybe save some sacred books, find secrets in some forgotten manual. It would have been proper for him to return out of unselfish devotion. He reminded himself of loyalty and duty. He hoped he was not returning because of sentiment, or nostalgia, or love. That wasn't supposed to enter into the master-student equation. As he neared the mountain, Saihung stopped himself from speculating. He sensed that he might actually be capable of forgiveness, that he was going back primarily for his master's sake.

It took him more than four weeks to reach Huayin train station from Pittsburgh. The tiny station seemed shabby, dirty, and poor. Certainly, compared to the terminals in the West, it was a mere ticket booth and turnstile. But it was the first tangible sight of the familiar place where so many of his past journeys had begun and ended. Beyond the crumbling building, Huashan rose up in expansive and grand proportions. Its lower flanks were hidden in cloud; it might have been an island floating in heaven.

Living rock. Pure water. Pines that reached inspiringly upward. For the first time, his perspective included his experiences in the United States. There was no immigrant struggle here, no thought of family life, no fighting with midnight hoodlums. Only rock, water, trees, and light. But oddly enough, he did not feel relieved to be back.

As he reached the summit of Huashan, he recognized uneasily that the mountain itself had changed. There were dramatically fewer monks. No one stood guard at the gates, no one was cultivating the fields, no one was attending to the altars. The ridges were eerily deserted, buildings and pavilions were abandoned. The legendary hoofprints of Lao Tzu's ox had been chiseled away. Soldiers had invaded the mountain only two months before, forbidding ceremonies, desecrating shrines, sending monks away. Huashan had not been invulnerable to political power, nor the barrels of guns. There were no monks to call the gods from the stars, no monks to keep the five elements flowing. No one was left to speak holy words that would resonate within the earth and sky. The air felt strangely cold, sterile.

The uninhabited temples were already crumbling from disuse. Some had been wrecked by vandals. Halls once fragrant with sandalwood incense now smelled of urine. Offerings of flowers and fruit lay withered on bloodied altars. Gods had been smashed or shot or stolen. Walls where holy song had once reverberated were now covered with obscene graffiti. The shrine of Lu Tungpin the Immortal, a small brick building with slender columns, was battered open. Doors lay splintered in the dust. The life-sized figure with its face of pale marble and royal robes of silk was gone. Sculpted eaves had been broken off, gilded figurines with gold and pearl dresses had been stolen, stone likenesses of mountain gods, sacredly nameless, had been catalogued for museums.

He imagined that he could still hear the footsteps of hundreds of men, the clatter of rifles, the barking of orders, the tearing of robes, the splitting of doors. In the cramped, abandoned rooms, he still could see the olive-drab men crowding blue-robed ascetics; he almost felt slaps and blows. He found a tattered poster, a political diatribe against religion, an appeal to join the glorious revolution. Shell casings littered the floor. Charred furniture lay in the courtyards.

He understood at last what the old masters said about the fragility of the human endeavor: Delicate spiritual attainment evaporated in the hellish world. Had he not come himself, he would never have accepted that this rare and extraordinary sanctuary was fading with barely a trace of notice by the outer society. Huashan had been, for him, a near utopia. How shocking to realize that human troops could march into heaven and turn it into something earthly, vulnerable—a minor bit of history to be concealed by petty bureaucrats and never learned by school-children. It was what the ancients meant when they said the Tao had abandoned a place.

In the past, he thought, the world was in accord with the Tao. The ancients regulated human life so that all were sensitive to the movements of the Way. Holy men should have been protected, not made into farmers, historians, bureaucrats, nor workers. Their existence was not a result of decadence, and, with their poverty, they could not have been accused of exploiting the economy. Social equality did not need to demand that every standard be leveled to the lowest one. But he knew that traditional ways were currently regarded with ignorant suspicion. Huashan's defilers had bullied gentle men, leaving only wrinkled old priests not worth a bullet.

Saihung trudged past the Jade Maiden Peak, through the last narrow canyon that led to his master's temple. When he got to the walls of the compound, the gates had been left strangely open. Saihung went into the littered courtyard, where a bronze incense burner had been overturned. He saw several pairs of shoes, and finding it odd, went closer to inspect. Inside he found sheets of paper with writing. The soldiers had torn holy writings apart, had placed them into the shoes, and had forced monks to walk on the words that they most revered.

He ran up the steps to the main hall, hopeful that his master had escaped injury. The Grand Master was capable of many unusual things, but Saihung knew that resisting gunfire was not one of them. He went into the deserted building, ignored the desecration of his childhood holy environment, and called loudly for his master. He was relieved when the Grand Master walked quietly out, his two acolytes standing behind him.

His master still seemed vital and walked unbent. His silver hair was impeccably combed, his face calm and dignified. He looked at Saihung steadily, wordlessly, as the light caught his eyes. The middle-aged acolytes, their hair beginning to gray, looked pale and anxious. They seemed uncomfortable in an altar hall without gods.

"Master, I'm back," said Saihung as he knelt upon the stone floor. Saihung indicated gifts that he had brought, but the old man regarded them indifferently.

"There's no longer a need for etiquette," said his master with a graceful wave of his long sleeves. "The world has changed."

"Are you unhurt?" Saihung shifted a little in place. He had not been on his knees like this for years.

"Don't worry," smiled his master bravely. "I've seen dynasties and nations fall."

"But this is different. It's a way of life. It's Taoism," Saihung frowned.

"Everything has its time. Then it must move aside for the next stage. The Tao is creative and relentless. It is everflowing. One mustn't try to interfere with it. The circle goes on. It cannot be resisted."

Saihung stood up and greeted them. He looked at their traditional robes. He was a shocking contrast in his Western clothes, short hair, and sneakers. His master was quick to notice his thoughts.

"Even you've changed," commented the Grand Master.

"But not inside, master!" said Saihung with emotion.

"Inside?" queried the master, smiling slightly for the first time. "You still need to clarify that."

Saihung was silent.

"If the Tao changes, so will you," continued his master. "Accept that. I've always told you: Your destiny will lead you on many distant journeys."

"I wish I could come back here." Even with the carnage, he was glad to be with the men who had raised him, who represented nearly infallible wisdom.

"There is no Tao here. Taoism is dead."

Saihung was stunned.

"The Tao is eternal." The Grand Master looked at him dispassionately. "But the Taoism I practice has been destroyed. They've forbidden me even to meditate and they would rather I died. But I will not go so easily. If I die, it will be my way. That choice is still open to me."

"Is spirituality at an end?" asked Saihung.

"As I know it, it is," replied his master. "But the Tao continues on. It is still something for you to follow."

The master turned away, and the acolytes followed in automatic unison. It seemed to Saihung that the old man was always turning his back to leave. For once, though, Saihung regarded this odd habit with some sympathy. His master evidently felt comfortable enough to indulge in old habits. It was a silent approval, for he knew Saihung would arrange things.

"Go with your brothers," said the Grand Master from the door. "Prepare for our departure."

Saihung turned to the two acolytes, Mist Through a Grove and Sound of Clear Water, and they bowed to each other solemnly. But as soon as the Grand Master was gone they smiled broadly and welcomed him. Saihung was quizzical. It always seemed that the acolytes laughed whenever they saw him. He was uncomfortable with the thought that they still saw him as the boy they had reared.

"How is it in America?" asked the husky Sound of Clear Water excitedly. "Is it true that the streets are paved with gold and that everyone there is rich and happy?"

"Yes, is it true?" said Mist Through a Grove, the elegant leader of scripture recitals. "Though I hear that some of the Westerners can be quite savage: They have the tails of foxes and they eat their young!"

Saihung looked at his elder brothers with amazement. They had guided him, taught him, advised him, and punished him as the Grand Master's direct representatives. They had once been his tutors and he had been the naive one. Now the situation was the opposite. What could he tell them? How could he say that he lived in a country that barely tolerated yellow-skinned people, and had places just as desperately poor as China?

"It's not like that, brothers," said Saihung gently. "There is no gold in the streets. The place is like here. Everywhere, people are rich and people are poor. The United States is no different."

The two acolytes looked confused. Saihung realized that they had never seen a newsreel, never heard a radio, never read the newspaper. They were true renunciates, innocent and pure. He felt dirty next to them, but somehow he did not regret it. He felt it better to see the world even if it soiled him. Being so innocent would have made him feel insecure.

"I'll tell you about my experiences," said Saihung. "But I have come a long distance and have climbed all the way up this mountain."

Sound of Clear Water rolled his eyes at Saihung's pleading look. "Have we ever known you not to be hungry?"

"Coming back makes me comfortable," joked Saihung.

"Come on, Little Butterfly," said Mist Through a Grove. "We kept some steamed bread on the stove."

The acolytes attended to the administrative necessities of holy life, and Saihung was back to do the same. There were a myriad of responsibilities that required attention aside from the colorful pageantry of festival days and the spectacular hours of meditative triumph. Duty required devotion and will to achieve. Discharging responsibilities was also the Tao. Simply to let things flow of their own accord was impractical, idealistic, and shallow. Following the Tao certainly meant understanding change and flow, but the course of things might be changed by a simple act.

After snacking with the acolytes, Saihung went to his master's chambers to estimate the scope of work to be done. He walked into the rough and tiny cell. Whitewashed walls reflected a soft and gloomy light onto the dusty tile floor. The only furniture left behind by the soldiers was a meditation platform and a desk. Both were too big to carry down the mountain. They would also have to leave them. All that would go would be small personal items. The Grand Master had designated a few clothes, his books, robes, a prayer rug, and a carved wooden statuette of his personal deity as the only things that he wanted.

Saihung left his master and went down the trail to see how his meditation hut had withstood the invasion. The small whitewashed building was still standing on the cliff's edge. He went in, picked up a table that had been knocked over, and sat down on the cold brick bed. The floor was gritty under his feet from dirt that had blown in. Dead leaves lay withered in the corners. It was quiet. Not even the whisperings of the wind were audible.

He found it difficult to accept the impersonality of Huashan's demise. He looked toward the temple, where he once had directed his prayers.

"The soldiers have done their jobs," he prayed to the night. "They believed that they were fighting for whatever good life Communist ideology represented, a new world without the dominance of hierarchy. But they destroyed one symbol for the sake of other symbols. The will of the people has been imposed upon Huashan, but the will of the people has no intelligence. It was not strategy; it was not reasoning."

He looked into himself, no longer with the formality of prayer rug and pyramidical meditation posture. Had he been able to fight, had he been able to hate and rage and pit his might against soldiers, the alienation he now felt would have been forestalled. Even defeat was better to him than this sense of helplessness, this mute necessity to accept circumstances. At least that would have been personal, more like the essence of the old order, where supplies were carried up the mountain by men, craftsmen made wares by hand, and painting, poetry, song, calligraphy, were all individual endeavors, and even a duel had an opponent to whom one was introduced.

But the modernity that had finally swallowed Huashan was faceless. Already, he not only felt that his holy land— that special place where a personal association with the divine could take place—was negated, but that he himself was to become increasingly anomalous in modern times. There was no room for an individual in times that were impersonal, uncontrollable, and incomprehensible.

The day of their departure was cold and clear. There was snow in patches, and small icicles dangled in the blue shadows of trees. The wind blew steadily across the pale vault of the sky, the distant rivers were lost in haze. The four of them walked calmly out of the monastery walls. The Grand Master was borne by porters and a sedan chair, his students followed on foot. No one was there to see them off, nor secure the broken gates.

Saihung and the two acolytes each carried backpacks of clothing and a few possessions. Their real problem was a heavy wooden trunk that held the master's personal deity and many old books. Saihung and Sound of Clear Water suspended the trunk by a pole and carried it between them. But descending Huashan meant descending vertical towers of granite.

"You go first," Saihung said to Sound of Clear Water. He let the acolyte lower himself hand-over-hand down an oxidized chain.

"I am at the next section," the acolyte called back in a while. Slowly, Saihung lowered the trunk by rope, the wood banging against the stone, the rope burning his palms. He thought of Uncle Poon, and wished that the old man was there to tie the ropes.

The trunk pulled at him, and his arms and shoulders ached from the load. He looked up, blinking to keep the sweat out of his eyes, saw only blue sky. He glanced behind him for a last look at his beloved mountain, but could not concentrate with the mighty swinging cargo in his hands.

"I've got it!" The rope suddenly went slack, and Saihung leaned back against a boulder in relief. He glanced at his master, merely a dark profile in a sedan chair. Mist Through a Grove, standing with the porters, urged Saihung to go on.

Saihung tied his pack on and swung himself down the chain. He scrambled toward the trunk that was a mere speck below him. The next one to descend was Mist Through a Grove, and finally, the Grand Master in his sedan chair. If he was frightened to be suspended over a gorge by ropes and the brawn of four porters, he gave no sign. Saihung watched anxiously as the fragile wooden container brought his master down the first cliff of the mountain. They would have to repeat the procedure over and over again before they would reach less dangerous heights.

Lingering ice made their job all the more dangerous. Both the porters and Saihung had to brace themselves against whatever tree or outcropping was available; sometimes, they even tied themselves to chains and iron pegs to prevent plunging thousands of feet.

It was afternoon before they reached the pavilions where pilgrims had once paused to have meals and tea. Halfway down the mountain, they stopped at one of these places so that the bearers could renew themselves. The

Grand Master walked to the edge of the terrace with Sai-hung. Below them was the rushing river that had its source on the South Peak.

Saihung had a sudden feeling of nostalgia. He had grown to manhood treasuring these walks with his master, had been able to mark the passages of his maturity by the memories of certain conversations. He unhappily contemplated a future without such talks.

"The Tao is like that river." The Grand Master seemed to be unaffected. He gestured toward the cataracts. "But don't think that following merely means drifting."

He reached out and pointed to the water. Below them, the stream continued to flow downward. There were rocks that had barred its way for centuries. It overran them and continued its course. "What if that rock was not there?" continued the Grand Master. "Then the course would change. What if we place more rocks in the path of the water? The course would change again. Sometimes, we can change the course of things merely by removing or placing obstacles. Sometimes, when confronted with obstacles, we must go around them and adapt."

The Grand Master reached out again, but this time toward Saihung. He blessed him. Saihung glanced briefly at the man he most cherished in the world, and for a moment, he felt the normally stoic master smile at him in benediction. It was the last time that they would stand together on Huashan.

As they waited at the train station, Saihung saw that his master never turned to look at Huashan again. They boarded the train crowded with gawking peasants, ducks and pigs, and rude conductors. His master was firmly silent. The warmth of that brief moment on the mountain had faded.

They took a train to Beijing, a journey that would take them days on the inefficient train system. Though it had been frigid on the mountaintop, it was just beginning to warm on the plains. Trees had sprouted their season's leaves, peasants were already at work cultivating the fields. The fields outside Beijing were flat and the crops meager. There were signs left from the war; some buildings still lay blasted apart, bomb craters had become fish ponds. About fifty miles from the capital they got off the train and were met at the station by an old bespectacled man and his servants.

"Master! Master! How good to see you!" said the thin man eagerly.

"Not at all, old friend. It's kind of you to extend your hospitality," replied the Grand Master.

Mr. Chen was a wealthy scholar, a retired professor from Nanjing University who had been an admirer of the Grand Master for many decades. He had a villa outside Beijing and, for the moment, was still lucky enough to have property and servants. His spacious mansion was the epitome of the scholar's home: oriented to the south, high garden walls, meticulously pruned trees and flowers, graceful architecture of carved eaves and peaked tile roofs. He led them to a guest house just beyond a gazebo and an enormous reflecting pool. The Grand Master was welcome to stay there as long as he liked.

The sky began to cloud over until it was an opaque gray. From horizon to horizon, it obscured the sun and sky. A harsh north wind blew into the pavilions, shaking the budding willows. The streams and ponds shivered with ripples. There were no birds.

A few heavy drops came on the crest of the next windy wave. As the Grand Master and the two acolytes walked beneath a covered garden path, their robes fluttered like flags on a mountain peak. Saihung pulled his coat around him, even as he carried the trunk. The sudden arctic temperature made his face pale.

The guest house was nearly as cold as Huashan, although it was much more ornate in its appointments. The plaster walls were painted a pale lavender, and the sandalwood lattice windows were a warm accent. Heavy, elaborately carved rosewood furniture stood around the room. The scholar's own paintings of peonies decorated the walls. Saihung and Sound of Clear Water set the Grand Master's trunk down on the thick carpet. That was all there was to represent their beloved mountain. Without speaking, they all knew that reality was only within. It was true that the common person needed props as memorials, but not even the mind of the greatest meditator could retain a whole paradise.

The rain quickened until it was a heavy downpour that sent unbroken rivulets streaming off the eaves. The constant percussion became a loud hiss. The plants of the scholar's garden did not endure the beating unbroken. Leaves and buds, never fully opened, fell to the ground and drifted forlornly in the black puddles.

Saihung walked down the outside portico, watching the curtain of rain, the slashing white of falling drops. Water was pure, his masters said. It washed away evil, and evil could not cross a running stream. Water washed the body. Water nourished the body. Water, in its patterns, formed an endless cursive calligraphy full of messages for the wise.

He had crossed the Pacific, yet the scars from his time in the United States were with him still. Huashan was rich with streams, yet evil had spattered its purity. He had brought his master to this temporary haven across rivers and through rain, but he still had a sense of foreboding and apprehension.

He walked back to the guest house and found his master also staring at the garden. The intricate lattice cast an indistinct lace of shadows on his face.

"It's done," murmured his master softly. "Those times shall not come again."

"There shall no longer be that kind of enchantment," agreed Saihung, turning to look out the window as well.

"Enchantment?" repeated the Grand Master. "No. There is no longer magic in this world."

"How did magic ever leave this earth?" wondered Saihung aloud.

"The folly of man, of course." His master brought a finger up to stroke his beard. "Steel. Electricity. The gun. These three things and the perversity of humanity killed all magic. It was in reaction to this that the Twelve Sorcerers met on the mystical island of immortality that we call Peng Lai. This island can never be found floating on an ocean. It does not exist in the ordinary world but rather on the plane of pure consciousness.

"They came from all over the globe to debate. They refrained from arguing, each one advancing his opinion. The sorcerers knew that they had power enough to fight, but decided against it, for triumph would be meaningless if the planet was destroyed in the struggle. Instead, they decided to withdraw all the mystical creatures, all the esoteric knowledge, and all the power into the depths of the earth. There they are, races of people, entire species of enchanted animals, all abiding underground with the Twelve Sorcerers.

"All know full well that the logical outcome of the present civilization is destruction. After that, the earth will have to go through thousands of years of purification.

Then, when man's presence has dissolved completely, magic will return."

The Grand Master paused, folding his hands. He looked into the heavens with the same devout expression that he had at an altar.

"Everywhere they rush to build homes and tall buildings. Across wildernesses, they string miles of electrical wire. Beneath the earth, they bore impractical tunnels. The skies are violated with planes, oceans polluted with wastes. What is their hurry? They are only suffocating the earth. Do they imagine that the only useful thing about this planet is to exploit its resources? If they understood the ideas of emptiness and impermanence, then they would see that virgin wilderness also sustains them.

"A person was made to fit into nature. In the forests and in the mountains, there are ten thousand forces that can sustain you at any single moment. The whisperings of eternity are audible, and nature nourishes through all five elements. Water, Wood, Fire, Earth, and Metal rotate in their proper orbits. We derive our power from attuning ourselves to it.

"But people imagine that wood is only good for building and burning. Fire is only to drive machines. Earth is only to be exhausted for its treasures. Metal is to make tools of destruction. Water is only to receive civilization's defecation. They think all that exists is what we see. They feel that nourishment is only what they buy in a store. They think all they need to attune themselves with is ambition, greed, and selfishness. They glorify their pettiness, but if they would only stop to think, they'd realize that they would be lost without their pathetic society. This world sustains them. When their time is up, it will swallow them mercilessly.

"Of all the creatures on the planet, only humanity was made to reason. Animals go through life without ever separating from their natural destinies. They live by instinct.

"Human beings should use their intelligence to turn away from their instinctive lust and greed, and turn their faces to the sun of holiness, the light of divinity. When the bright Way appears, one should be moved to reverence. Instead, man has used his cunning to glorify his senses and cater to his greed. In the holy light, they shade their eyes and cling to the shadows."

The Grand Master turned to Saihung.

"This is your last lesson in China," said his master.

Saihung nodded solemnly.

"It's important to understand how to cope with life. Taoists understand life in a certain way. We have evolved a philosophy as an approach to life. But this philosophy will not always work in another culture."

"The West is completely different from China."

"I know. But when you are in the West, you must try to understand it. Don't simply try to stay Chinese. Blend in with that culture. Understand it. Every culture works. When you are in it, you must do things their way."

"It's difficult to remember all that I am. In America, I am sometimes immersed in conflict. I cannot always keep my composure. You are telling me that these times are evil, yet you tell me to blend with it."

"Why be complicated?" asked the Grand Master. "*Yin* and *yang* and the ten thousand things mean separation. Separation means discrimination. Discrimination means discord. You must not cling only to the positive. In life you must also accept the negative. Those who do not accept both sides are the ones who become angry. Life is an oscillation between good and evil. Let it oscillate. There is creation and destruction, good and bad. Life will proceed on its own. Try to blend with it. Remain simple."

"How can I?"

"I know how you live," said his master with a slight tone of reproach. "But though you must blend, you must also remember who you are within. Search for your destiny. There are no more soothsayers. One must prophesize one's own destiny. That is unique. Who says that the only way to seek Tao is on a mountaintop? The Tao is change. Every day new people are born. Every day, people die. If people didn't die, nothing would change. It is people who change and so they imagine that there is progress. Past, present, and future all coexist. Movement in life is natural. The question is, where are you in this movement?"

"If only I knew . . ."

"I will not tell you. I'm not you. Your god is within you. Your god is your self. That is the source of your destiny."

"But I no longer have access to the teachings of our sect."

"You are afraid. That is unbecoming. If you give in to fear, you are like common people who do not understand the Tao. Hatred and anger come from fear. For the common people who are bound in such emotions, enlightenment comes only at the moment of death. Then their eyes and mouths open wide in amazement. They want to act, but death takes them just a moment after realization. You don't want that. You want your enlightenment while you can still act upon it. Put aside fear. There must be faith."

"But how can I now seek my enlightenment?"

"Life is but a wisp. It will be gone in a flash. Try to get as many moments of enlightenment—little realizations, tiny insights. Build up. The Tao is not fixed. Neither is enlightenment."

The master scrutinized him. "There is ambition and drive in you. That means you are incomplete. Some mystery drives you."

"But I don't know what it is."

"Of course not. That's why it's a mystery. If a man's life could be reduced to a road map, it would be quite worthless. You're a human being, in all your complexities and mysteries. Your personal scripture is inside you. You must decode that for your realization. I know you feel cheated. You want to become an immortal. But that art is trivial compared to the more essential issue of *why*? Why do you exist? Or do you even exist? If you can answer the why of your existence then you have found your purpose. Your time with me was merely preparation. Your life is the time to exercise your learning. Spirituality and realization are personal. Practice through your whole life to gain realization. When you gain that realization, it should be cherished, treasured, and hidden. Keep it to yourself. Once you understand, you will see that whether you are priest or waiter is immaterial. These are only identities."

Identities. Saihung pondered that carefully. All his life, he had sought to wrap himself with the reassuring mantles of various identities. He had seen the noble, classical characters of his grandparents and had sought to emulate that. He had idolized the Grand Master's powerful understanding and had aspired to the same heights. He had abandoned more roles than other men had ever contemplated beginning. Student. Warrior. Politician. Priest. Scholar. Actor. Acrobat.

"I do see that clinging to the roles of the mind can be a detriment," offered Saihung.

"You recognize that to a limited degree already," agreed the Grand Master. "You reject the fixed identity of these various roles. But there is one final role you still cling to: your self. Only when you can leave that behind can you say you have glimpsed the Tao."

"Master, you do not know what it is like out there. I must believe in myself to survive." He could see no practical way to live in the United States in a state of self-lessness. The tension between the simplification of the self and self-belief worried him.

His master seemed to lose patience. He turned away from Saihung. "So? Am I supposed to be sympathetic?"

"If only I could have more of your guidance. If only you would let me come back. I'm sure that I could leave all those roles behind."

"That is impossible until you fulfill your task," said his master severely.

"Why don't you and the acolytes come to America? I would work day and night to support you. Only please do not abandon me."

"Can our link be affected by distance?" asked his master.

"I am not so strong that I can know the Tao with no further teaching. I am only a tenth of the way there." He meant it.

"I made it. You make it." The Grand Master turned to look at him. There was a fierce look in his eyes. "Do you think I am going to make it easy for you? My masters never did me one favor. I had to achieve everything on my own. You have no time to indulge yourself any longer. The world is swiftly moving toward the dark side, but you are still attached to your idea of your self. Go! Go and explore and experience the world. Only when you are world-weary will you realize the answer that I need to know. Until then, you must strive and suffer and persevere like everyone else. No one carries another being along the Way. No one."

Saihung did not dare to say any more. He knew he would have given anything to avoid going back to Pittsburgh. But he could not argue with the orders of his master. He withdrew to stay with nearby relatives. The Grand Master was under surveillance by government cadres and to stay too long in a group encouraged suspicious investigation.

Saihung walked through the front gate of the estate. He opened a bamboo and oil-paper umbrella against the rain. The clouds were dark, dense, moving swiftly. A sound like a thousand drumbeats came from the umbrella. He looked up. The clouds were like a mirror of the ocean. In the deluge, it seemed like an entire sea was falling on him.

SIX

No Song to Sing

Saihung returned to the United States with fresh memories of China. He could still see twilight's last rose rays on white stucco, indigo shadows of poplar trees angled across yellow dirt threshing floors, brilliant green gourds hanging from bamboo trellises. He retained the impression of old men playing stringed instruments, not caring about an audience, only the pleasure of playing as they sat alone in doorways. He remembered smoke from distant fires against cobalt skies, even cherished the memory of walking through the straw and stubble of fields. The images were vivid in him. Even in the apparently barren fields, he was aware that so much was alive, the trees, the wind—breath of nature—small frogs in the field, birds, flies, a snake.

Time was slow in China. It was a pulse beating a muffled, unhurried pace. A day was a mark anywhere; but in his culture, the cycle of change was double what it was in the United States. The division of hours was two times sixty minutes, so that people only divided a single day and night into twelve periods with poetic names. The months followed the cycle of the moon. The year was thought of as twenty-four seasons, and people looked expectantly to the fulfillment of that particular time: Coming Rain, Big Heat, Little Snow, Beginning of Spring. No rushing—working hard, yes, sometimes being hungry, or caked with dirt blown by a yellow wind—but at least life was honest and direct. People lived close to the earth, an ear to the slow rhythm that was a gentle echo of one from deep in the planet's core.

Life was faster in Pittsburgh. The earth was paved with asphalt and concrete and stabbed through with steel posts. Trees and nature were relegated to precise holes in the suffocating pavement, animals were categorized in zoos. Men rushed in buses and cars to their appointed eight hours a day. Eight hours. A job. Numbers. No poetry. Eight. Be at work at eight, work for eight, under the glare of fluorescent light, in the wind of a forced-air system, with clothes of chemicals, eating foods that had probably never breathed, or walked, or felt tender roots in the grainy anchorage of soil.

Was home to be a kitchen of familiar foods, a new family that spoke with voices from the homeland? Of black hair, round faces, amber skin, onyx eyes, laughter? A dumb joke with an untranslatable pun, stupid, innocent, and just like home. Food was food, but that special feeling just of talking, forming delicious syllables from childhood, playing roles observed from elders, pulling together in tragedy, making that special gesture indicated by a custom so ancient as to be genetic—all this was the special seasoning that was fragrant, maddening, that made eyes roll heavenward in delirious remembrance.

For the Chinese in Pittsburgh, their hearts and often their families were across the ocean. They still unwittingly followed a pattern begun in the nineteenth century, when men came to the United States for the railroads, the gold mines, agriculture, and fishing. A few had been kidnapped, others came just desperate for money. Through the decades, fleeing poverty, they worked to earn their fortunes. Some dreamed of returning as rich men. (One can still see ostentatious Greco-Roman structures in southern Guangdong built as self-monuments by those who succeeded in realizing their dreams.) Others worked to bring wives and families to the West.

No one escaped the dichotomy of homeland and workland, the difficulty of having love and value far away. All held the idea that hard work and sacrifice would enable them one day to realize their dreams. Saihung fell into the same immigrant pattern. He, too, sent money faithfully back to support his master and the two acolytes, for he was now their primary source of income. He, too, labored under the idea that he was working for some deferred goal while separated from beautiful memories by an ocean.

Even when Saihung got up on a Sunday morning, he kept thinking of the landscapes of his childhood, of happy moments in his grandfather's garden. He went into the backyard. Warm air with a trace of the river's scent flowed around him. The peach tree was almost in full leaf now, and he noted with satisfaction that it seemed healthy. Behind him, Uncle William slammed the back screen door, and walked down the path to the garage.

Uncle William was a portly man in his late sixties, with a round head, graying hair, and silver stubble on his rough-skinned face. He called Saihung to help him with the car. He never let anyone touch his Buick, but Saihung obliged his elder anyway. The older man simply enjoyed displaying the centerpiece of his possessions. Though he called Saihung to close the garage door, it was evident that what he really wanted was an attendant for what was to him a nearly royal event. Uncle William wiped the fenders carefully, and checked the whitewall tires. Methodically, he raised the hood and checked first the radiator and then the oil. Satisfied that all was in order, he climbed into the driver's seat and started the car carefully.

The gleaming, jade green car rolled into the sun, and Uncle William drove it through an alley to the front of the house. Saihung was left to close the door and return to the house to announce that all was ready. Aunt Mabel, wearing a gay and colorful dress, took up a picnic basket and went out to the front.

In this short time, Uncle William had already turned the car off. It wasted gas to leave it idling, he always explained, before warming it up again. No matter how often Aunt Mabel urged him to keep the car running while he waited for her, he kept them waiting as witnesses to his exactly timed five-minute warm-up period.

The first stop was always the dairy near Schenley Park. "Again?" exclaimed an exasperated Aunt Mabel. "We always have to go for ice cream! Every Sunday, it's always the same!"

Aunt Mabel, a rather large-boned and formidable woman, liked to complain. Married to her for over forty-five years, Uncle William adopted the archetypal male strategy: silence. He knew when to keep quiet—he had often whispered to Saihung that it was this sense of timing that was responsible for his long marriage—and there was no ultimate argument as long as he was driving. Saihung kept quiet too. He liked ice cream.

All three had their cones at the dairy. Despite her complaining, Aunt Mabel seldom failed to get ice cream. Her favorite was strawberry, though she and Saihung often experimented with the many available flavors. Uncle William was a true classicist and staunchly ordered a double vanilla each and every time.

Uncle William had worked in restaurants nearly all his life, first as a waiter, then as the owner of several unsuccessful ones. Retired, he still worked from time to time in restaurants during busy seasons. He always insisted

that he could have run his own business, but his individualistic temperament and his unwillingness to compromise were his undoing. Had it not been for the financial
help and planning of his wife, he would have easily slid
into poverty as he chased his dreams.

It had been Aunt Mabel who had first urged a retreat
to China during the 1929 depression, shrewdly waiting
until it was again economically advantageous to return.
In the years that followed, she earned her living as laun-
dress, eventually opening her own shop on East Ohio
Street. They had bought several pieces of property with
her savings, which made their retirement more comfortable. Uncle William was thus spared the knowledge of
whether his dreams could stand an ultimate confrontation
with reality. He was content to tend their properties—
disinterestedly—and ride around the North Shore in his
Buick. This was something that he loved to do, for he
loved both the town and his car.

As his aunt relaxed, she took on an almost girlish demeanor. During the week, absorbed with taking care of
the house, property, and Uncle William, she often seemed
distracted and worried. She had once been a very stout
woman of peasant proportions, but had begun to stoop and
shrink in her aging. The laundrywoman's constant soak-
ing in water had encouraged an arthritic condition that
had twisted her hands painfully and had pulled her body
inward. Saihung massaged her frequently with liniments
of every conceivable nature, but there was no reversing a
lifetime of exposure. Years of hard work showed on Aunt
Mabel's wrinkled face, graying hair (which she permanent
waved but refused to dye), and bent spine. Only when she
was out on Sunday did she seem to cheer up. She smiled
and laughed, gazing happily at the deep green trees.

Panther Lake was a small reflecting pond in a city park. There was a monument to George Westinghouse at the far side of the pond. This semicircular art deco screen, painted gold, looked strangely similar to monuments in China. There was a sculpture of a boy facing the bas-relief screen in a central and symmetrical fashion. Large rocks lined the pond, like the gardens in Beijing or Suzhou. Golden carp swam languidly in the water. Irises, weeping willows, and magenta-tipped Chinese magnolias lined the shore. A warm, honey-colored sunlight washed down through pines on the hill that overlooked the tiny hollow. The benches were massive black granite in simple post-and-lintel arrangements. They had no way of knowing whether the garden's designers had intended such an oriental feel, but it suited their nostalgia.

Aunt Mabel laid out the picnic basket. She helped Saihung and her husband to the lunch of homemade dim sum (small dumplings steamed with various fillings), and poured tea from an old chrome thermos. Aunt Mabel enjoyed serving them, liked watching them appreciatively devour her creations. But once the lunch was over, she walked over to another section of lawn by herself to sit and look at the flowers and, Saihung knew by the faraway look in her eyes, dream of her life back in China.

Sitting on a granite bench, looking up at the sky through bright willow green, he could feel the cool stratospheric breezes as they had been on the summit of Huashan. He could hear the clean water rushing over rounded stones, and smell subtle fragrances of pine, earth, and sandalwood incense. There had been haughty cranes, regarding him with avian disdain, monkeys trying to steal fruit from the altars. There had been kindly old men who had inspired him to grasp the knowledge and art of living in nature. They had drawn him to know himself through meditation. They had instilled an awe for life and had then expanded that to the dizzying exploration of contemplative space.

Huashan had represented all that he had valued of tradition. He remembered the many religious relics on the mountain: begging bowls, rosary beads, scrolls, and books that were so delicate that he had to use bamboo tweezers to turn the pages. Huashan had been his unbroken link with the past, his image of antiquity. He was part of a continuous lineage, in touch not just with his master, but with a living tradition. As long as he lived, that inner link would last, but he still envied the churches and cathedrals around him, the news stories of religious relics being moved with great devotion: a bit of a saint's clothing, a tooth of Buddha, a desert scroll. Many people throughout the world had their beauty, the object of their worship. He had nothing but himself and memories of his old country.

Home. The soul needed a home. For unless it could fly to some safe haven, it could not be itself. The place didn't need to be a fancy structure, just a special spot where there was a sense of safety, comfort, and most of all, belonging. There, undistracted by speculation, ambition, wondering, or fascinations, in a place so instantly familiar as to be nearly transparent, the soul could be naked. Divesting itself of all outer attentions, it could abide in its primary nature: a state of total self-absorption, of purely conscious being. Home was not a house, but his heart. It was in the core of his body, the interior of his tabernacle. His body was home, his mind was home. Perhaps never again would it be in the China of soft hills, budding magnolias, rivers barely cognizant of Emperor Yu's influence. Never again would there be a holy land to run to, flee from, pick up weapons to defend, kneel in the humblest reverence to worship. His holy mountain was gone, lost to tourists, conquered by the ignominy of weather station and defense radar placed on the highest point, trampled by young pathetic iconoclasts who saw antiquity as their parents' world to savage. How smug he had been, always believing Huashan was there to go back to! He had taken it for granted.

He smiled, and then sighed. He knew that he had been given the means to understand and overcome the situation. He had been taught that externals were insignificant to the real qualities of inner cultivation. The masters would have burned temple, relics, even their own robes to demonstrate what they had taught him repeatedly: The Tao is to be found within.

He was determined to preserve his spirituality. He resolved that he would earn enough money to make himself independent. Huashan might be gone, but he would still maintain its legacy. He looked at Uncle William, strolling on the opposite bank to feed the fish. He turned to his left. Aunt Mabel was pretty in the afternoon sunlight, sitting on the grass, arms and head propped on her upraised knees. They were living as successful and gentle an old age as they knew how. Saihung wanted that too, though that did not mean a Buick and a wife. He wanted to pursue his quest, fulfill it, and return to his master.

He began a new job at a restaurant named Lotus Garden. It was quite far from Foreland Street, across two rivers. He had to walk a mile downtown to catch a bus that would take him to the South Shore and the community of Brentwood. The restaurant was on a busy highway, one of the main thoroughfares to Pittsburgh from southern Pennsylvania.

Situated between an auto repair shop and a glass shop, with an ample parking lot in between, the gray brick building must originally have been a simple rectangular box building, like all the others on the semi-industrial strip. Now it had fake oriental tile roofs grafted on to its roof line, and window frames with some flimsy version of latticework. Both the eaves and the frames were painted with shiny green and red enamel. The owner of Lotus Garden was apparently modern and progressive: He had a large illuminated sign proclaiming the name of his establishment, the letters written in a silly Chinese calligraphy style. Below it was the legend, "Gourmet Chinese Food."

The interior was quite dim, even dark after the glare of the streets. Only a bit of sunlight came in the front door and two windows that faced the street. A slightly pudgy man came to meet him. He was vain and combed his hair back with just enough hair dressing to impart a smooth sheen. He was taller than Saihung, and left the impression of an athlete gone slightly to ruin. Boss Lee was in his late thirties, only a few years older than Saihung. In culture and temperament, however, his prospective employer was quite different. He was Saihung's earliest encounter with the Americanized Chinese.

Boss Lee had grown up in the United States and did not expect to find his life's fulfillment by going back to China. He was a shrewd and ambitious businessman, but his expectations of success were a home in a good section of the city and Western education for his children. He was a proud veteran of the U.S. Air Force, and liked to affect a leather bomber jacket. A few pictures of him and his Flying Tiger were hung behind the counter.

The restaurant was one long narrow room. Green vinyl booths lined the walls. Square tables, set on the diagonal, and covered with white tablecloths, filled the center of the room, and there were several large, round tables for banquets. Aside from a monstrous stainless steel station for refilling tea, there was little else on the walls except for a few token paintings and a single audio speaker softly playing big band music.

The kitchen was a small room, painted a shocking chartreuse mitigated only by years of scrubbing. Saihung saw that there were four woks and stainless steel prep counters, sinks, and a dishwasher. The equipment did not seem to be enough to support the room, but Saihung refrained from voicing his judgment. At least the kitchen was very clean, he commented to Boss Lee. His employer told him that the city inspected the restaurant more often than white-owned businesses. Bribes were part of the cost of doing business.

Boss Lee introduced Saihung to the head chef, but Saihung already knew him from the rumor mistresses in Chinatown. The cigarette-addicted cook was named Devil Lee. Notorious for his bad moods and vicious tongue, the women at Big Mrs. Lee's store viewed him as pure evil. An ugly man with a crooked mouth, his face had been badly scarred in a fire. No one had called it an accident. They all said the gods had marked him as a monster as a service to humanity. Devil Lee's main perversity was refusing to cook when the mood struck him, often at the time when the restaurant was most busy. He grudgingly shook Saihung's hand and blew a stream of smoke into the air.

At four o'clock, Saihung changed into his uniform of white cotton shirt, black pants, and bow tie. Within two hours, the room filled up astonishingly quickly. All the patrons were white, and most were from the neighboring wealthy districts. Some came even in chauffeur-driven limousines. They were greeted by the maître d', a slender and obsequious Japanese incongruously named Big Duke. Most of the customers had favorite waiters, and asked Duke knowledgeably for the table in their preferred sections. They were equally certain about their favorite dishes: egg fu young, chow mein, pork chop suey, won ton soup, sweet and sour pork, moo goo gai pan, egg rolls, barbecued spareribs. Those who considered themselves connoisseurs ordered half a roast duck with gravy. Children often ordered from the "American" menu, and had jumbo shrimp, barbecue pork sandwiches, or chicken gravy sandwiches.

The youngsters not only liked the strange versions of home cooking, they liked two waiters in particular. The waiter Lee Shi had a large pointed head, greased-down hair, broken nose, and a normally rude disposition. He lived with the sorrow of his only son's death. A bullet shot in the air during a village celebration came down into the crowd, striking only the youngster. Lee brooded constantly about this accident and had lost all his faith in the future. He was savage to customers and workers alike, and it was only with children that he ever smiled or expressed a gruff consideration.

His confederate was the oldest one there, dubbed Ancient Lee. No one knew his exact age. He dyed his hair (Devil Lee always accused him of using black shoe polish), and kept it combed in a cresting pompadour. The sides swept into shiny fenders above each ear. When it got hot, a long strand fell down one side of his face, and he loved to fling it upward with a flip of his head. He looked like he had no neck, and his shoulders were hunched up. He liked to make jokes that the children loved, but that no adults understood. He never laughed at them either.

Saihung did his best with the tables left to him. Already an experienced waiter, he took the orders and delivered them as promptly as Devil Lee would cook them. The sound of the restaurant reached deafening levels, as patrons talked, babies cried, and the waiters shouted to take orders. Each time that Saihung hit the swinging double doors was like a drumbeat, each time that the porcelain plates slid across the steel counters was like the clanging of gongs. Devil Lee, his lips firmly clamped around a drooping cigarette, kept four woks roaring with sizzling food, his iron spatula moving like the piston of a train. Whenever the cook lifted a pan, yellow flame shot up to the fan hood, steam burst from the boiling sauces, and fragrant aroma exploded into the kitchen. The pace was maddening, with Devil Lee shouting for orders to be taken, the waiters yelling for new dishes.

Two dishwashers worked furiously in the corner. During the day, these two black women shared in the hard work of mopping the floors, setting up the tables, receiving supplies, and preparing the food for the evening crowd. They carried supplies down to the basement where there were additional stoves to pre-cook the ducks and chickens, tables to peel and cut vegetables, and even facilities to sprout mung beans and make bean curd. During most of the evening, they kept steaming hot water streaming over the heavy plates and bowls.

Bessie was thin, with large eyes and a completely anonymous demeanor. She crept into work each day, like a mouse walking tentatively across a room. She spoke to no one, did her job impeccably, and left promptly at quitting time. But her partner was her complete opposite. Her nickname was Lucky. She easily weighed three hundred and fifty pounds. She took short steps on enormous barrels of legs, and her girth and body were so large that she moved through doors at an angle. A trip to put away dishes left her breathless, and she piled dirty dishes close in the sink so as not to let them get beyond reach. Lucky took a special liking to Saihung. Even in the heat and the clamor and the frantic pace of the kitchen, she sang gospel songs at the top of her voice. Perhaps because Saihung was the youngest one there, she always gave him a wink and a reminder that it was "never too late to accept the Lord."

The bins were emptying rapidly; there were no more ducks hanging in the oven. Devil Lee rushed down himself for more supplies, leaving the next batch of orders unfilled. The waiters complained, and Boss Lee frantically rushed into the dark basement. Lucky went too, and in her haste, slipped at the top of the stairs. Down she fell with only a tiny scream.

There the two of them lay at the foot of the stairs. Boss Lee was nearly unconscious. He was plump, but he had not been able to withstand the hulk that had fallen on him. Lucky lay winded on top of him. Lee Shi, Ancient Lee, and Saihung went to the top of the stairs. The pair had fallen back against the door to the downstairs storeroom. Before the waiters could act, the door opened. All the spectators looked hopefully down for additional assistance. Devil Lee looked down at Boss Lee as the former war hero rolled his eyes up in supplication.

"Oh, it's just you making all that noise," said Devil Lee in annoyance. He slammed the door, banging the proprietor's head a second time.

The waiters hurried to the bottom of the stairs and dragged Boss Lee up. He had been fortunate enough to escape with only a sprained ankle. Then they turned to Lucky.

"Can you get up?" asked Saihung.

Lucky's eyes rolled around. "I need help," she wheezed.

Lee Shi and Ancient Lee, ever resourceful, rushed into the storeroom and found some rope. They looped it around her waist and pulled until Ancient Lee's pompadour had collapsed over his face like a curtain.

"Come on Kwan, do something!" cursed Lee Shi.

The only implement Saihung could find was a snow shovel. He quickly put it under Lucky.

"Pull!" commanded Saihung as he pushed down on the shovel.

"Hurry!" he shouted again as he heard the handle split and the metal buckle. With an effort, the two waiters pulled the dishwasher upright and helped her up the stairs for some tea. Ancient Lee shouted to the cook to get back to work, but with a restaurant full of customers, Devil Lee decided that he would take a break. Everyone shouted at him, but he strolled out the back door. The dazed Boss Lee had to fill in until the temperamental cook returned to the fires.

Saihung lived at the restaurant for weeks at a stretch, only occasionally going back to his attic room in Uncle William's house. There was no way that he could keep his practices a secret, but he openly exercised only martial arts and stretches. This was something that the other older men accepted readily, but not for themselves. Saihung soon discovered that they might watch what he was doing, even applaud it, but they were too lazy or tired to learn from him.

Morning exercise was a tradition in China. One could see people old and young alike practicing in the parks of China, and their exercises were not games or singular activities like running, but martial arts and *qigong* (the art of breath control).

Saihung began his exercise day by washing. This simple procedure was equally important as scripture or meditation. Hygiene contributed to purifying the body, and the masters had taught him that divine energy would move on its own if impurities and obstacles were removed from his being. One obstacle was as bad as the next, and it did not have to be mystical or obscure. Saihung washed his face. He washed his eyes with cold tea. Ears were cleaned with a damp cloth, and he cleaned his nose and throat with warm salt water. In an adaptation of the techniques that he had learned in India, he inhaled the saline solution and spit it out his mouth. He cleared his throat by gargling and coughing up any phlegm.

"It's a disgusting habit!" exclaimed Ancient Lee about Saihung's gargling.

"What about your spitting?" retorted Saihung as he wiped his face.

"Now I suppose it's all that sniffing next," continued Ancient Lee, referring to Saihung's breathing exercises.

"Leave him alone," broke in Lee Shi. "Ox Boy needs the exercise. Why deny him if he wants to follow the way of the ancients?" He turned to Saihung. "Go on. Don't listen to that old thing."

Saihung just smiled and went into the empty restaurant. He pushed back the tables to give himself some room. His fellow waiter's banter did not irritate him. It was an oddly comforting routine.

He tied a long sash around his waist to restrict the meridians. He went through a set of *qigong* that featured long inhalations and exhalations in coordination with low squatting stances and vigorous arm movements. This particular set was called the Eighteen Luohan Qigong, and was a Buddhist martial art exercise that he had learned in the school of his primary martial arts teacher, Wang Ziping. Saihung did not care if he was a Taoist practicing a Buddhist set. Every technique was valid. The only difference between the success of one system and another was how much the practitioner trained in disciplined earnest. The masters adopted whatever was effective; an over-emphasis on distinctions was contrary to the Tao.

Qigong was control of the breath. It led to control of the body and mind. By training the breath, waste gases were expelled from the body, blood was richly oxygenated, and the meridians were regulated, enhancing not only the immune system, but bringing equilibrium to the mind as well. This was accomplished not simply through the opening of energy pathways to the brain (the Taoists believed that both sides of the brain would simultaneously open if the practitioner cleared all breathing passages and meridians), but in the very act of deep breathing itself. The mind became calm whenever the breath was held, and energy accumulated where the mind concentrated un-waveringly. Saihung's breathing exercises were the very prelude to health and spirituality.

The exercise was more elementary than the levels of practice that he had attained on Huashan, but this did not matter. Since the Taoists did not believe that health and spiritual attainment were permanent, the mind and the body had to be constantly maintained. Negligence and en-vironmental stress could tear down one's development even faster than progress could be made. Reaching high levels of meditation made it all the more necessary to maintain physical health because the hypersensitive mind could be disturbed by any unbalance. Ultimately, there was to be no distinction between body and mind. His en-tire being was to be kept in harmony. The Taoists ignored neither the physical nor the metaphysical. That was their genius.

Once Saihung had accumulated the energy of his *qi*—that force formed by the synthesis of air, nutrition, and the transformation of his very hormonal essence—he had to circulate it throughout his body. He did this through martial arts, and one of his favorites was Bagua, a martial art form based on the eight trigrams of the *I Ching*.

Lofty in principle, deeply philosophical, tied to the deepest Taoist theories of the channeling of energy, Bagua (literally, the Eight Trigrams) had a rather scandalous origin. According to the oral histories of the martial arts world, Bagua had been introduced in the nineteenth century by the master Dong Haichuan. He was a handsome and notorious playboy, whose adeptness at martial arts saved him continually: He was always fighting the champions of the women he had seduced. He had learned his art from two Taoists, one named Shadow Under the Moon, the other named Shadow Under the Lamp without a Shadow. Other than their names, nothing more is known about his teachers—and knowing the Taoists, those were undoubtedly not even their true names.

The next history records of Dong is that he became a eunuch in the Forbidden City—whether through a desperate attempt to flee the law or the punishment of the law itself is unclear. He then kept his identity a secret until the emperor saw his skill at maneuvering through a garden party without spilling his tray of tea. He was ordered to demonstrate, and from that point on, Bagua slowly came into the open. Dong eventually trained seventy-two disciples.

Its full name, Bagua Zhang, meant that it was a palm system. Its exponents used only the palms to strike, seldom a closed fist. It was a more vicious pugilistic art than mere boxing, for the palm fighter achieved his effects by issuing his *qi* at the moment of impact. In the same way that a healer sends his energy into another person for therapeutic reasons, the Bagua boxer sends his to rupture organs.

But not all martial arts were practiced solely for destruction, and it was this unique dual nature that made Chinese martial arts special. Bagua had excellent results for its proponents. Since it was exercised by walking vigorously in a low squat around a circle while performing mock boxing moves with the arms, it stimulated the internal energy within everybody.

The energy could be harnessed, increased, and directed if one knew the methods. It could be used for healing, killing, or meditation—it only depended on the motivation of the practitioner. Since it moved in circles and spirals, not in a linear fashion, Bagua's circling and spinning movements stimulated the internal energy to spiral upward, nourishing the entire being.

Bagua was based on the eight trigrams of the *I Ching*. This classic was well known in Imperial China, and is still a popular book today. Ancient in origin, the book began its basic speculation with two simple lines, one straight, and one broken. The straight one represented *yang*. The broken one represented *yin*.

The early sages formed a rough symbolism of their basic metaphysical ideas by formulating a set of lines whereby all possible combinations of the broken and unbroken lines were ordered in groups of three. These eight combinations were given names. All straight was heaven. All broken was earth. One straight on the bottom was thunder. One straight at the top was mountain. One broken at the bottom was the wind. One broken at the top was lake. One broken in the middle was fire. One straight in the middle was water. In this way, abstract symbols were correlated with the most basic natural phenomena that the sages could observe.

In order to arrange this grouping, they incorporated the directions. Fire was placed in the south, where the life-giving heat of the sun came. Water was placed in the north, where the cold north wind and the snows originated. Heaven was placed in the east, for the rising sun; and earth was placed in the west. The other trigrams were then arranged around these to form the intermediate directions such as southwest, southeast, and so on. By doing Bagua, Saihung was performing a movement art based on these very ideas.

His raising of the internal energy was also expressed in terms of the trigrams. In this way of analyzing his inner process, he imagined heaven in his head, earth at his perineum. His heart was fire. His kidneys were water. He could easily see that the process of raising his internal energy was symbolically expressed by the broken lines of earth gradually being replaced by one straight line (water), then two straight lines higher in the body (fire), until the all straight lines of heaven was achieved. Symbolism and actual physiological change were thus intermixed in his practices. In his mind, it was difficult to distinguish whether the practices proceeded from the speculation of symbolic calculations, or whether the trigrams were merely borrowed to express empirical discovery. His masters would not care for such a speculative question. In their minds, symbolism and reality were always interrelated because everything in the universe was a microcosm of something larger.

Saihung then practiced other martial arts that suited his mood for the day. His favorite was the Lost Track Fist, but he also reviewed his knowledge of such forms as Xing-yi, Tai Chi, and the forms based on the movements of animals in a nearly shamanistic way: Snake, Monkey, Crane, Panther, Tiger, Mantis, Eagle, Dragon. His experience in Sandusky Park as well as other fights that he had been in on the streets of Pittsburgh had convinced him that he could not abandon his martial arts. He never knew when he would be challenged and he never wanted to be caught unprepared. He never expected that his next fight would be in the restaurant itself.

One of the patrons who always asked for a table in Saihung's section was a large heavyset man with a shaved head. He came weekly with his wife, a quiet and shy brunette. The man ordered the same dishes with religious regularity. Eggroll, egg-drop soup, sweet and sour pork, fried rice. With identical regularity, Devil Lee would get the order wrong. The man always wanted lichee instead of pineapple with the pork.

One night, as patron and restaurant went through this ritual, Saihung engaged the man in conversation. Saihung had never forgotten the habit of sizing a man up. There was no doubt that this six-foot heavyweight was a fighter. It was clear in the way he walked, the way he dominated the tiny booth, even the pugnacious way he ordered his meal. He had the air of one who had been in much combat. Saihung felt sure that he had seen the man elsewhere.

"I know who you are," said Saihung one night in a casual tone. It was late, and Saihung was tired from working. When he had remembered where he had seen his customer, he had forgotten propriety.

The wife looked with concern across the table. The man looked up with annoyance.

"Now who do you think I am?"

"You're the Batman." The Batman was a masked wrestler on TV. Saihung and the others sometimes watched on Saturday mornings as they washed the floors.

"How the hell did you know that?" asked the Batman. "No one is supposed to know my true identity."

"It's not hard."

"Well, I didn't think you were so smart."

"There's a lot you don't know," replied Saihung. He immediately regretted it. It had been a hard day. He had argued with Devil Lee.

"You shrimp!" roared the Batman. "If you're so smart, how come you can't get my dinner right?"

Saihung threw down his tray in exasperation. The restaurant suddenly became quiet. Saihung felt the sudden discomfort of having a hundred people staring at him. Duke and Boss Lee rushed over.

"Is there some problem?" asked Duke nervously. The Batman was fully a head taller than Saihung. Duke was ridiculously dwarfed between them.

"This is between him and me," shouted the Batman.

"Hey, anytime," replied Saihung.

"You?" bellowed the Batman. "What can you do?"

"Like I said before, there's a lot you don't know."

"Don't fight!" urged Boss Lee in Chinese. "It's bad for business."

"Don't fight, Edgar, honey," said Mrs. Batman.

"Edgar?" snickered Saihung before he could stop himself.

"Hey, watch it!" growled Edgar Batman.

"Look. I've had a long day," said Saihung. He tried to remember what they said in movies. "Either put up or shut up."

"Why you punk!" cried the Batman. "I could flatten you so fast."

"Come on! Come on!" yelled Saihung, shaking his hands at his sides.

Edgar Batman charged Saihung. It was not a sight that Saihung took heedlessly—seeing a man both wider and taller bearing down would give anyone pause. But Saihung had always loved testing his mettle in combat. Whether he would win or lose depended on his skill and his experience. That was why he fought.

Saihung sidestepped and threw a palm blow into the Batman's lower abdomen, but he pulled the energy. It would not be good to rupture a customer's stomach, but it might be nice to have a little fun. The big man went up on his toes as if he had had an electric shock. Saihung quickly reached under the armpit and threw him.

As the Batman rolled, Saihung jumped up and rolled with him in a perfect somersault. As the disoriented Batman pitched to the end of the throw, Saihung was right there beside him. There was a brief instant for Saihung to grin triumphantly at the dazed giant before his swift elbow strike knocked the Batman unconscious.

"So sorry! So sorry!" apologized Duke to the other customers.

"Ai!" exclaimed Boss Lee. "You'll drive all my customers away! Quickly! Revive him!"

Saihung did as he was told. In his training, it had not been enough just to learn how to knock a man out. He was also taught how to revive and heal people. He sat the Batman up with some effort. The man was heavy, and his head filled Saihung's hands like a huge bowling ball. Saihung massaged his neck and then slapped him hard on the back. The loud whack brought the Batman back to consciousness. Saihung brought the Batman back to his table and helped him into the small booth. He saw that Mrs. Batman was too concerned to speak.

"I'm very sorry," said Boss Lee. "It won't happen again."

"Forget it," panted Batman. He turned to Saihung. "How did you do that? Show me! Show me!"

Just then, Ancient Lee tottered out with the Batman's order. There were still pineapples instead of lichee, but the Batman took it in good humor. Since the Batman had become so friendly, Boss Lee made no reprisal against Saihung, and the other staff members were happy just to have a break in the routine. They told Saihung that they had all earned regular customers who requested them by name. Each one of them had a story. But none, they told Saihung, had been impressed because they had been knocked out.

Saihung laughed, but inside, his thrill always gave way to introspection. That night, Saihung thought over his encounter with the Batman. He had fought with a man known only by a mask. Soberly, he knew that the fight had not been necessary. Perhaps that kind of contest had been excusable in his youth, but now he began to see that it was so much egotism. By fighting, he had exposed a little bit of his own identity. He had also exposed, at least to himself, his own arrogance. He thought back to the meditations that he was striving to master just before he had left Huashan. He was supposed to be erasing his ego, he thought. It would take a great deal of hard work to overcome this tendency of his.

Hard work. Over the years that he was at Lotus Garden and among the Cantonese immigrants of Pittsburgh, he worked hard not simply at his job, but at his practices as well. He began to see a fascinating parallel between the persevering habits of his coworkers and the perseverance demanded by his sect. If there was a single tenet that the immigrants had it was a word that is inadequately translated as "struggle," with the added connotation of "work hard" and "ability to bear suffering." It implied that one who knew how to "struggle" would succeed in the world. That was the way both of the immigrant and the ascetic. Struggle, suffer, work hard, until success came.

From the moment that he saw this common cultural element between holy and worldly life, he found much greater comfort in the Chinese community. After all, except for the differences in their goals, they were all struggling for a future that held out no promise of reward. In a way, the society of men in the restaurant was almost monastic, and leaving the restaurant was as fun as leaving the monastery on festival days had been.

In late fall, Saihung joined his uncle and aunt on a rare outing to the countryside. Uncle William drove his reliable Buick to a beautiful spot over a lake. Big Mrs. Lee and her family, and friends of his aunt, Jean and Henry Chan, joined them. All along the shore, the maples were turning into a crimson only seen on the rarest of silks. The women unpacked plenty of homemade dim sum, along with tea and beer. There was much laughter as they ate, but Saihung was moody and quiet. His aunt suggested that he go off by himself. She understood his moods, and understood the importance of solitude.

Saihung excused himself and went down to the water's edge. On a whim, he rented a rowboat. Gripping the thick oars tightly in his fists, he made a few tentative dips into the water before he fell into the rhythm of pulling and pushing. The blades made regular sweeps into the blue-green water, and soon the bow of his boat sliced the smooth lake in a perfect path.

He put his whole body into the rowing. His legs steadied and tensed with regularity, his abdominal muscle contracted and rippled with each stroke. His back muscles pulled, tested themselves against the thick water, and his arms pumped gratifyingly with blood.

He found himself breathing to a regular cadence. Like *qigong*, rowing became a special art of breathing. At least in its physical aspect, this rowing was almost as good as the art that he faithfully cultivated. It filled his lungs with clean, sweet air, excited the nerves and blood vessels of his body. Who cared about esoteric technique? This was still giving him health and experience.

The water was placid, calm. He looked at the ripples as they fell away from his boat. Abstract lines shimmered for a few moments, then faded into nothingness. Like the Tao that allowed some facet to come to the surface only to withdraw it again into its depths, the wake of his boat was constant, but never the same. It came into existence, it passed from existence. There was no emotion. No anthropomorphic interpretations. No words. No vision. Just him and the water that was like the Tao.

Soon, he had a sensation of his body meshing perfectly with the movement of the boat, with the swaying of the water, the gentle undulation of the lake. He remembered his master's words, that life was oscillation. There was creation and destruction. There was movement. He had to blend with the life, just as he was doing now.

Rowing a boat was so simple. Rowing wasn't exercise, a game, a sport, or a religion. It was just rowing and thus it was his perfect Taoism. He rowed on. Pulling. Pulling.

Serenity passed into him. "Enter stillness." These two words were one of the most sacred mantras in Taoism. He became aware that his rowing was silently repeating this mantra. His oars dipped again and again. They entered and rose. Entered and rose.

He hadn't meditated for a long time. How could he, working and living in Lotus Garden? But now, unexpectedly, he recognized himself falling into the familiar state of meditation. Somehow, the outer experience of rowing on a lake reflected inwardly in him. His outer senses were stilled and he found himself looking inward. Certainly, his eyes still saw, but his mind saw only within. His mind stilled, his soul emerged, beautiful and pure. He became like a dazzling white swan gliding over the dark waters.

Meditation wasn't otherworldly. It wasn't separated from life. It was life. It was living. Only in meditation did he recognize freedom and absolute being. Only in meditation did he remember that being a waiter was making a living, and not living.

His spirit intact and shining, he reached the shore and beached his boat. He walked into the woods. Saihung had always loved forests. Perhaps, he considered, he had been a forest dweller somewhere in a past life. Whatever the explanation, he knew that the feel of unobstructed earth beneath his feet was a great comfort, and the feeling of trees surrounding him made him feel safe.

He thought over how naive he had been when he had first come to the United States. He had expected Iroquois and Sioux, hunters, cowboys. He had thought of trees coming down to the water. How could he have known that America was a country that did away with its past? In China, nothing was thrown away with evolution. People lived substantially as their ancestors had. America was not even two centuries old yet. In China, there were family bloodlines, guilds, restaurants, farming methods, and schools of painting that preceded Columbus's discovery. He could not have known that things changed so quickly and thoroughly here. The America he had come to expect through books was gone. Perhaps Uncle Poon had been right to curse him. He had been too idealistic.

The woods were quiet. Sunshine fell gently down through parted boughs, birds sang intermittently in high-toned warbles. Listening to them, he suddenly remembered a very special song. This was not a composition made for entertainment, but a mystical one of sacred syllables. It was a song for people interested in mystical history. If one went to a particular place and sang the song, then the guardians of that place had to show it to the singer as it had been in the past. Time would be pierced—it was only in nestled circular layers anyway—and the beauty that had once been would be revealed. It seemed a little like making water flow backwards, but that was exactly what the song did.

Saihung had used it in China. History for him had thus not always been the reading of books, but the nearly direct experience of having seen it all. He had seen poets, warriors, the Seven Sages of the Bamboo Grove. He had seen things as clearly as the trees before him now. Time, he had been taught, could flow in either direction. He decided he would sing this song. He could begin to learn from the natural world of this place, absorb the softly blowing wind, the pristine water. He could find the Tao anew here.

He sat for a time in contemplation, an inner ablution, a turning to the sacred. Then he stood, and in the gestures and movements that accompanied the words, sang the song. The wind stilled. The birds stopped. Even the trees trembled in response to his voice.

He waited expectantly. Nothing.

He reviewed his procedures. It had been a while since he had sung, but it was not a melody easy to forget. He sang again. Still no response.

By the third attempt, he understood that the song would not work outside of China. Some things were tied directly to a place, his master had once told him. Certain types of spiritual practice could not function outside the place they were formulated. He realized in sorrow that this was now the case. There was to be no revelation. This kind of spirituality would not work away from Huashan and China.

He stood helplessly. Discouraged and sad, he turned toward his boat. As he rowed back to the waiting picnic, he realized his boat ride was just a boat ride.

SEVEN

Child of Peace

Saihung returned to China in 1963. Hearing that he was going to the homeland they all cherished, many people gave him red packets of "lucky money." Big Mrs. Lee, Uncle Feng, Uncle Poon, Ancient Lee, even Devil Lee gave him something for his journey. Saihung was moved. Even on Huashan, there wasn't this kind of support and camaraderie.

The reason for this trip was a request from his last surviving martial arts teacher, Wang Ziping. A prominent martial artist, he was known throughout China for his patriotic duels with foreign champions. He had always been viewed favorably by the Communist government. When Mao Zedong wanted to improve the people's health with martial arts, Wang was among the masters invited to reveal their arts.

Wang Ziping had accompanied Premier Zhou Enlai on a diplomatic visit to Burma. Saihung had no doubt that it had been Zhou's own expert sense of diplomacy that had led China to utilize martial arts as a tool of international relations. He suspected that Zhou was secretly sympathetic to many classical things purged in ideological conflicts. But characteristically, Zhou did not champion anyone's cause if they were being attacked. Instead, he waited patiently until he could resurrect the people and ideals that he wanted. Keeping his motives hidden, never showing his loyalties to anyone, he kept people guessing until it was impossible to undo the groundwork that he had laid.

Saihung felt that Zhou was behind this new interest in martial arts or, as it would come to be called in the West, *wushu*. The encouragement had all the hallmarks of the premier's manipulations: He liked strategies that even his enemies would have to applaud. Improving public health was a noble ideal that no one could quarrel with.

Wang was born in 1881 in Hebei province. Originally, neither his father nor his grandfather favored his interest in boxing, even though the two of them made their living as professional fighters, teachers, and bodyguards. Wang trained on his own by lifting rocks. He became a trouble-maker, and stories tell of his banishment from his home-town for being a "boxer bandit." That might have been the end of his talent, for without a master, it was impos-sible to become a martial artist. Brawn and courage were not enough. One also had to have technique and even the financial support of a school in order to have the time to learn.

Wang had an exhibitionistic character, however, and this is the way that he found his teacher in 1901. Boast-fully demonstrating his might to a group of onlookers, Wang had used his bare hands to stop a large water-driven millstone. After that feat, a man stepped out of the crowd and offered to accept Wang as a disciple. Wang had knelt immediately, the traditional sign of respect for one's teacher, and had become a student of the famous Yang Hongxiu.

Aside from duels fought within the confines of the mar-tial world, Wang Ziping was publicly known for his ex-hibition matches with foreign strongmen. From the in-vasion of China by the British during the Opium War, through the humiliation inflicted on them by the Western allied powers in 1900, and the Sino-Japanese War which began in 1927, until the founding of the People's Republic, the Chinese national character had suffered a tremendous inferiority complex. Wang became a hero by standing up to foreigners. Today his exploits may seem xenophobic, but one cannot underestimate the emotional scarring that happened to those of his generation. Until the mid-1940s, Wang accepted any challenge that came from Westerners or Japanese in fighting bouts well-documented in the journals of the day.

Wang was enormous. Over six feet tall, he had a massive body of sculpted muscle, huge hands with fingers like steel claws, and feet like battering rams. A devoted Moslem, he usually wore an Islamic cap. But there was nothing spiritual nor even merciful about Wang. He had the beard of an elder, the face of a no-nonsense knight. His eyes had an unalloyed severity and he seldom smiled.

He was hot-tempered, disinclined to be kind. Prior to the 1949 revolution, martial artists in China were an elite class, virtually a law unto themselves. Wang was an authority in society by virtue of his physical prowess and chivalrous upholding of morality. However, it also meant that he could act out his anger whenever it suited him. Fighting was a daily certainty whenever Saihung accompanied Wang, for the master kept his skills sharp by brawling with street thugs. If anyone got in his way, or touched him slightly, it triggered an unreserved rampage. In China, where the streets were crowded and the majority of people walking the streets were rude, there was no avoiding such confrontations. Saihung suspected that it was a situation Wang secretly enjoyed.

That temper also expressed itself in restaurants. Wang loved to eat at banquets—after all, his devoted students were required to pay. Many were the times he would be offended by the poor quality of the service. He did not hesitate to express his irritation, no matter how minor the infraction. Countless times, he overturned an entire dinner table with one push before stalking out. His embarrassed students had to file out behind him, paying for the damage without complaint. The journey back to the school was always doubly traumatic: Not only did they have to endure Wang's anger over whatever offense had happened at the restaurant, but they also had to bear his displeasure over being hungry.

Saihung and the other students stayed with Wang out of duty, of course, for in those days the Confucian standard of loyalty to one's teacher was still intact. But their loyalty was reinforced because they wanted to learn from one of the supreme fighters of his time. Ironically, Wang Ziping's name meant "Child of Peace." Elders frequently gave children lofty names, even references to virtues that were absent, in an effort to correct character defects. Wang lived up to his reputation, but not to his name.

In prerevolutionary China, supremacy in the martial world was decided solely by dueling. If a young martial artist killed or at least humiliated an older one, he or she added that master's prestige to their own. Wang was not simply a street fighter, but a respected prince of the martial world. With a famous name and an established school, challengers came nearly every day to try their skills against his. Among the most formidable of the fighters that Saihung remembered was a Shaolin boxer.

This fighter had been clearly confident of his ability. When he strutted into the gymnasium, even the more experienced boxers moved aside. He had a body like an inflated anatomy chart come to life. Every muscle was clearly defined, and rippled with a palpable intensity when he arrogantly stripped off his shirt.

"Forget it," Wang scoffed in response to the man's request for a match. "You'll lose."

"I insist!" The fighter took a raw coconut and shattered it by gripping it in one hand.

Wang laughed derisively. He turned to his students. "Watch closely. I will show you something you've never seen."

"Attack when you like," Wang said as he faced his opponent. His politeness was sarcastic. The man charged and Wang struck with a strike so rapid that Saihung almost missed seeing it. The challenger paused.

"A weak strike!" He stepped back to puff up his chest. "I am unhurt! I've practiced the Iron Shirt for years!"

"No so," said Wang with a cruel smirk. "Look!"

The place where Wang had struck, just above the nipple, suddenly showed a dark spot. Gradually, both the fighter and the students watched as a fearful dark cloud of hemorrhaging blood blossomed across his chest. A sudden pain shot through the man and he collapsed—still looking at his own body.

"Heal him!" Wang had told his students as he had walked from the room.

Wang also sometimes lost these impromptu fights. One of the most spectacular times took place at his school in Beijing. When the gatekeeper had announced the entrance of a challenger, all the students expected a quick resolution. But this time, when Wang Ziping looked up and saw a wiry man about seventy years old, he paused. Saihung stole a look at his master. A veteran boxer, Wang could size a man up at a glance. This one had skill.

The stranger was tall and quite thin. His white hair was cut into a severe crew cut, and he had a long beard, the symbol of an elder. He evidently spent a great deal of time outdoors, for his skin was as brown as teakwood. Saihung noticed that his arms were rather long, and his fingers were slender but flexible. Wang Ziping was over six feet tall and was a heavyweight. The man was like a stick figure before him, a virtual caricature.

"I know your reputation," began the stranger politely. He held his clasped hands gently before him in the gesture of respect. "But please understand me. I have wandered my whole life trying to perfect myself. I do not believe in isolating myself in a mountain retreat. I believe in testing myself against other skilled people. If I win, then I know that old age has not yet bested me. If I lose, then I know the weak points that I must still correct."

"I have heard of men like you," responded Wang. "You are interested only in the pinnacle of skill."

"My abilities are quite poor. I am not here to bring shame on your school, and I would understand entirely if you were to deny me. But I would only like to see if I have made any progress in my practices. Would you please oblige me?"

Wang could not refuse such a request. His honor was at stake.

They began to circle each other warily. Neither made any flamboyant moves. There were no fancy postures, no talking, no tricks. Just two old men who were fighting to see who the better was. They were two dedicated martial artists who would, if nothing else, uphold the dignity of the challenge and themselves.

From the very first clash, Saihung could see that his teacher was at a disadvantage. Blows that would have felled a horse were easily dodged or received by blocking forearms. The stranger's posture was low, his stance was strong. Saihung could see that he was using the Elephant style.

The main feature of the style was to use the hands like the trunk of an elephant. This meant that the arms were very flexible and came at a variety of unusual angles.

Whereas other styles might use open hands, chops, or jabs with the fingers, the stranger relied primarily on his closed fists. The Elephant style emphasized the Eight-Cornered Meteor. Instead of a simple punch, the style singled out every angle of the fist as worthy points of contact. Overhand raps with the knuckles, pounding attacks with the base of the fist, roundhouse swings with the thumb side, and use of different angles of the face of the fist were some of the variations.

Wang Ziping's style was the Lost Track Fist, a synthetic style that had derived its techniques by taking the best of all schools of boxing. Based on the Long Fist style, it also incorporated styles that mimicked the fighting of animals, as well as the internal styles of Xingyi, Bagua, Tai Chi, *qigong*, and meditation. The masters had collected entire schools of boxing into their repertoire. They had even used opium to bribe masters to reveal their most cherished secret techniques. When they had wanted to expand their kicking style, they had inducted all the techniques of the famous Mandarin Duck kicks. When they had wanted to know about fighting from the floor, they had taken the Dog style. They wanted so many techniques at their command that the opponent would be overwhelmed, or "lose track" of the fight. But that did not help Wang with his current challenge. It was still the skill, strength, and talent of the fighter, not the styles of the participants, that determined the outcome of a match.

The stranger hit Wang repeatedly, hard enough to make booming sounds, but not enough to injure him. A man with Wang's reputation was expected to be able to withstand some punishment. Saihung also saw that the man touched lethal spots, places that were used to kill. If Saihung could see it, he knew also that Wang Ziping could feel that he himself was being spared at every turn. The itinerant master was satisfied with demonstrating his abilities and control; he was not intent on hurting his adversary.

They fought in fifteen-minute rounds. Wang was tiring. He had already lost his Moslem cap in the struggle, and it was one of the few times that Saihung had seen him out of breath and sweating. The older man was not even breathing hard. He only went to an unoccupied side of the gymnasium to wait courteously for the next round. Wang Ziping tried every technique that he knew, including secrets that he had never taught his students. He still could not best his challenger. In all, they fought four rounds for a bout that lasted over an hour. It was the challenger who stopped the contest.

"Thank you for indulging me," said the man politely at the end of the final round. "You were too kind in letting me off."

"No, no. It is I who must thank you," responded Wang breathlessly. It was the only time in his life that Saihung had ever heard his teacher thank an opponent.

The man came close to Wang as he strode out of the school. "You should continue to teach. You are still good enough to do that."

Saihung had pondered the man's vast superiority. Totally anonymous, without career or students, the old man cared only for his art. Yet, nothing about his persona hinted at his attainment. True, he had a better posture than most men his age, and he walked in a way that was more vigorous than even young men, but nothing else hinted that he was so great. That was why, Saihung thought, one should not boast or demonstrate: There will always be someone unrecognized who will best the arrogant. But such humility was the last thing on his mind whenever he fought. Saihung had even challenged Wang Ziping himself.

Saihung had beaten a rich young fighter. Winning certainly was acceptable to Wang; in fact, it was everything. But the playboy was the son of a prominent official whose previous opponents had lost either out of deference to the father or because they had been paid. Only Saihung had ignored the convention. He had hurt the youth's body, but worse, had annihilated his pride. Wang had called Saihung to task.

"He deserved it," Saihung smirked. "I couldn't stand that weakling."

"Watch your language when you speak to me!" said Wang sharply.

"I'm not apologizing to his family."

"I order you!"

"Never!" Saihung turned to leave.

"Do not turn your back to me!" shouted Wang.

As Saihung reached the door he heard a whistling sound. Cocking his head just in time, he dodged a heavy ceramic brush holder. It shattered, tearing a chunk from the carved door. Saihung turned in a rage. He shouldn't have done it, but he attacked his master.

At that moment, a proud assessment of his own skill came into his mind. He could support six men on his shoulders and legs. He could snap a leather belt buckled around his biceps just by flexing. He had kicked in a two-inch-thick door through the acceleration of acrobatic flips. He could dispatch his opponents with a flying split kick.

"The man is fifty years older and I have more muscle," he told himself as he closed in with a combination of strikes. Not a single one touched Wang. Where he had been angry in discussion, the master was calm in fighting. He could easily have killed Saihung with a single stroke.

Instead, he dodged and blocked, content to test Saihung's knowledge of boxing.

This frustrated Saihung. He lost all his composure and tried dozens of techniques. Vicious blows to the groin, quick elbow strikes, jabs to the eyes. Nothing connected. As Saihung tried less and less honorable techniques, Wang began to hit back. His every punch hit a meridian point, and they hurt badly.

The fight went on for five minutes. That was too long, and Saihung knew he was in trouble. He finally had to use his proudest weapon, the flying split kick. It was a technique he had developed himself. From a standing start, he could leap to head level and flash his legs in a perfect forward split. With all the momentum focused in the front leg, he had felled numerous opponents. Saihung was desperate to salvage at least his pride. He drove Wang back with a flurry of combinations. Uppercut, cross, elbow, jab, palm. At the last second, he leapt high and executed the devastating kick with perfect accuracy.

Wang Ziping had never seen the kick before. But his reflexes were so fast that he did the one thing Saihung's previous opponents had never succeeded in doing: He stepped back. Wang reached quickly up and grabbed Saihung's ankle and he threw his student roughly to the ground with a strong twist.

"I will give you something to remember me by," said Wang savagely. He knocked Saihung unconscious, though Saihung blocked the punch with both hands.

It took him months to recover from the injuries that he had sustained in that battle, and only the constant supplication and intervention of Saihung's family and the Grand Master of Huashan patched up their strained relationship. It had been fortunate that Saihung had been able to continue his education, for one of the best things he eventually learned from Wang Ziping was fearlessness.

After numerous battles, any fighter could claim to be reasonably fearless. In spite of the great variations in personality, one might still predict most of the ways an opponent could react. Many fights were even won psychologically, when a fighter gauged his adversary's inner weaknesses and decided his best strategy. But Wang Ziping had taught Saihung fearlessness by pushing him onto an inhuman opponent, one who did not use the techniques created by the human mind. Wang had taken his class into the fields to find a herd of wild boar.

One by one, his students were required to fight a boar. Some succeeded, others had to be saved from trampling. It was then Saihung's turn. He was allowed to wear only leather gauntlets and shin protectors. Some elder students selected a mean-looking pig and goaded it into a charge.

It rumbled menacingly at Saihung. He was stunned at how fast the animal moved. For a moment, he could hear the low grunt, see the red eyes, smell its bad breath, as it aimed its tusks at him. Saihung dodged and struck at the animal, making an ineffectual sound that only made the boar mad.

The boar did not fight in any particular style. It had no strategy to guess at. It could not be talked into making a mistake. It fought on pure instinct and relentless anger. The boar came again and this time Saihung dazed it by striking just above its eye. This stunned it for a moment. It turned sharply, driving full speed toward Saihung. Using the power of its hind legs and shoulders, it slammed into Saihung's side, and gored a deep, bloody gash. It slowed to turn and Saihung grabbed at an ear.

There was a squeal and a surge of energy from the angry pig. Saihung could not hold on. He leapt up and elbowed

Wang Ziping as he looked in his eighties.

it hard to no effect. The boar retreated a little, but that was only to gain momentum for the next charge. The pig bashed him again. He was badly bruised and bleeding. The boar was not tiring, but was renewing its attack. Saihung knew that he had to end the fight. He hammered a double-fisted strike to the top of the boar's head. It didn't kill it, but it did make the boar pause in pain. Close to exhaustion, Saihung hit the animal ten more times. Confronted with such a madman, the pig lost interest and soon sauntered indifferently away. "Sloppy," Wang said as he looked at the breathless Saihung. "But at least you're still standing."

Saihung turned away in exhausted frustration. He looked over the few students who had survived the test with their pride intact, as well as the equal number who had been badly injured. Wang ordered them to return to the city. He did not say a single word of approval to the victors, and he rebuked the losers, even though they were all champions of bouts with men. That was the way it was with martial artists. They only knew harshness and they only looked at a person's weakness.

If that person were an enemy, then they were always forewarned of the possible attacks and counterattacks. If that person were a student, then they were always notified of their defects so that they could progress. Martial artists could be stark in their relationships. They were used to upholding a standard, and had staked their entire lives on never compromising. There was no such thing as praise or encouragement.

When Saihung arrived in Beijing, he was well-prepared to face his master. But he was surprised to find a considerably less expressive Wang Ziping. The man had become circumspect, even quiet. It was true that he was eighty-three years old, but he still was more robust and heavily sinewed than men a quarter of his age. Though his hair was completely white, his eyes still showed undimmed ferocity. Wang greeted Saihung formally and even more curtly than usual. He motioned with his eyes toward a little man in a green Mao suit. Saihung knew instantly that the Communist cadres would be surveying everything.

Saihung had no private time with his master. He instead concentrated on rehearsals and learning prearranged sparring routines with other returned students. Wang Ziping had trained so many of those who had been called for the demonstration that almost none of them knew one another. It was instructive that nearly all had now returned from outside China. Proud individualists, these martial artists had not stayed in China past the early 1950s.

Constantly monitored, the martial artists learned their routines in sullen silence. They disliked the restriction, but endured it for the sake of their master. They rehearsed at Wang's school, an old gymnasium with pale green walls and high windows that let in a bright, flat light. There were mirrors, punching bags, wooden men for target practice, ropes to climb, and acrobatic equipment. The air had a distinctive smell, a musty and pungent odor not from the training men, but from something in the building materials. They trained for eight hours a day under Wang's strict supervision. Each move was practiced repeatedly. If perfection angered the gods, then Wang was determined that they be madly furious.

The stadium was filled to capacity the night of the performance. Mao Zedong, Zhou Enlai, Zhu Deh, and other officials sat in a special box. Saihung looked at them skeptically. Once they had proclaimed martial arts as feudal.

Now they thought it might be useful for the sake of health and as a performing art to show to other countries.

The old martial artists came out to thunderous applause. There was the Monkey Master, who fought in movements inspired by apes; the man dubbed the Rat, who fought with a thirteen-foot cavalry spear. Wang Ziping himself showed his still vital skills by demonstrating the spear and the monk's spade, a heavy staff with a shovel-shaped blade on one end and a crescent-shaped blade on the other.

When it was Saihung's turn, he came out dressed in a simple blue cotton shirt, white cotton pants, and the domestically manufactured version of tennis shoes. He had a sash tied tightly around his waist. In rapid succession with two other students, he showed the double meteor maces, the double daggers, and the Swimming Dragon Sword Form—a style handed down by a woman who had tried to assassinate the Emperor Qianlong. The audience cheered at his every dramatic move. Saihung used his experience as an actor to add facial expressions that complemented his shadow-boxing routines.

Finally, his last solo performance came. He gripped a spear and looked out at the cheering crowd. Wang had not said a thing to any of his students, which was as close as they came to approval. The performance was going well. The leaders of the government seemed pleased.

His spear was made of the trunk of a young sapling. An inch and a half at the butt and tapering only slightly, it flexed gently whenever it was thrust out. The spear tip came to a sharp point, and its ferrule was wrapped with a long tassel of red horsehair that tossed eye-catchingly with every moment. The tassel was not just for show. In combat, it distracted the opponent from the tip, and it could also be used to trap other weapons. The style was named the Blood Spear, because the spearman started battle with a white tassel and let it be dyed with his enemies' blood.

He gripped his weapon tightly as his name was announced. "Kwan Saihung. Blood Spear." Saihung walked out onto the stadium floor. He stood for a second as the audience calmed down. The spear was straight, with its butt resting on the ground. Its white wood suddenly reminded him of a spine. He thought of his own spine, of the energy that he had been trained to raise in almost supernatural procedures. He brought his left hand over his head while he inhaled slowly. As soon as he gripped the spear with both hands, he raised it up mightily and launched himself into a performance that showed exactly how a man would fight. As if he was surrounded by many opponents, Saihung blocked, dodged, thrust, and leapt into balletic attacks. He wanted the audience to believe that he was actually fighting invisible enemies. Even Zhou applauded his performance. He wondered if the premier remembered him.

Other schools demonstrated before Saihung returned for prearranged sparring performances. Barehanded, Saihung faced the director of Wang's Shanghai school, a stocky, solid, crewcut man in his sixties. He held two real daggers.

"Attack!" shouted Wang. Saihung disarmed his opponent in five seconds. One: The man attacked. Two: Saihung dodged. Three: He hit the back of one hand. Four: He knocked the dagger from the other. Five: He returned to his ready position. The audience cheered.

"Too slow!" Wang cried. Wang, who had sometimes leapt into the ring whenever a losing student threatened to ruin the reputation of his school, wanted everything to be perfect for this event. He took Saihung's place saying, "Three seconds should be enough."

The dagger man attacked again. One: As he charged, Wang stepped into him. Two: He struck so rapidly with each hand that both knives dropped to the ground. Three: Wang was back into his original position. Not only did the stadium erupt in admiring applause and shouting, but Mao himself gave Wang an ovation.

As the performances went on, Saihung reflected soberly. Once, he had wanted nothing more than to be a martial artist. Growing up, he had seen former Imperial knights and had aspired to their heroism. But modernity and the second World War had forever changed what it meant to be a warrior. Guns and armies became more important than skill and chivalry. There were no martial artists as in the old days. Those who fancied themselves so were only romantic hallucinators. What was left was a special heritage that tough men like Wang or his instructor from Shanghai were trying to preserve.

Now the old arts were being sought by Mao and his government. The arts that the warriors had kept hidden were being exposed and exploited for political reasons. Of course, the decision had not been up to him. Wang had decided to cooperate, and Saihung had returned to China in obedience to his master's request. But he would not have exposed his art to the eyes of the curious under any other circumstances. He had always been taught to keep his skill hidden until the last possible moment. Yet from then on, the martial arts that represented principle, honor, discipline, and individuality would be transformed into a performing art and sport. They were giving away the legacy they so cherished.

EIGHT

Isle of Anonymity

Two days after the performance, Saihung took a train westward. As he traversed the countryside, he could see the makings of the new China: factories, a little more mechanization in the fields. The nation was on the verge of industrialization. It would be good for economics, the military, the balance of trade. He could see that people suppressed by his own former aristocratic class now had a chance of advancement. But with the passing of the old social order came the fading of the ancient, classical culture he so treasured. Imperial houses were now museums. Scholars were now working for archives if they were lucky, or in fields if they were not. Huashan itself had but a few monks and nuns (women were never occupants on Huashan in Saihung's time) imported by the government from other areas to act as caretakers of exhibits for tourists.

Young people look to the future, he reminded himself. Old people look backward to the past. All old people should disappear, he thought glumly. It wasn't right to stand in the way; it was actually unfair to both sides. There was no reason to bar the young from having the world the way they wanted it, nor was there any reason to stop the old from holding to their values. But in spite of his philosophizing, Saihung realized that there would soon be no place for him in his homeland. Nearly everything he valued had its roots in the nineteenth century and beyond.

Saihung disembarked at dawn from the train he had ridden for two days. He walked from the station to a lake. Waiting for the boatman, he stood at the water's edge, a tiny figure dwarfed by the sweeping surface of the water. Gray and blue profiles of distant hills and mountains could barely be seen against the overcast sky. The underbelly of heaven hung low, and the clouds seemed to bear down just above his head.

Across the lake was a dark, crown-shaped island. No other details were visible from the distance, just the punctuation of stone and tree upon the still water. He knew that his master was there—could even detect a subtle presence—but there seemed to be little other life around the lake.

As he stood for some time, a group of swallows swooped down over the pale water, diving and turning with acrobatic finesse. He wondered if they were returning from some nocturnal journey, or whether this was an aerial dance to greet the rising sun. With wings like swords, speed that took the eye and mind long moments to comprehend, they cut their eccentric paths and were suddenly gone. They had come only long enough to stitch a counterpoint to the pastoral scene.

He listened to the gentle lapping on the sand, the soft swelling impulse of the ripples. On Huashan, the impassive mountain had represented absolute stillness. Movement was hidden in its living caves, its subterranean streams. On this lake, there was still the combined image of stillness and movement. The calm surface was like the meditating mind. As long as there was solitude, there was a chance for the Tao to come. It had not died simply because ideologists, bureaucrats, and generals had decreed it. The Grand Master might still be nurtured by the Tao, and add to its flow his voice, love from the heart, and the dedication of his spirit.

The boatman arrived and, after some bargaining, agreed to pole Saihung to the island. He helped Saihung load the boat, asking if he was a merchant. Saihung only laughed, replying that he was a visiting relative. He looked like a homecoming traveler gone a bit mad. He had brought dozens of gifts, and he had been purposefully excessive: flowers, fruit, cone-shaped wheat bread, peanuts, pickled vegetables, dried tofu, noodles. The presents filled nearly the entire boat.

He was happy to see the two acolytes waiting by the tiny dock, standing in the violet shade of a willow tree. They had kept their long coiled hair and Taoist robes. He greeted them with a bow and quickly loaded them with his presents. For a minute, he felt a little awkward, even shy. He was glad that he had some props.

Sound of Clear Water dispensed with the elaborate ceremonial hand gestures and began giggling. Saihung stood awkwardly and uncertainly.

"You look odd." The acolyte pointed to Saihung's American clothes.

"Don't tease him," said Mist Through a Grove with exaggerated protectiveness. "He's a world traveler."

Saihung shifted uncomfortably. Why were his older brothers always teasing him? He didn't know what to do. If he was still the man from Pittsburgh, he would have shaken their hands, but that gesture was foreign in China. If he was still a monk, he would have bowed and gone through the elaborate rituals of greeting. If he was still the child they thought he was, he would have hit them both.

"This is the style," Saihung remarked defensively. "I have to fit in." In his mind, he began to see his fellows as country bumpkins.

"A Taoist concerned about style!" howled Mist Through a Grove, his topknot coming nearly undone. "I can see that you are truly progressing."

Saihung lost his temper and was about to begin brawling when all three noticed their master standing at the top of a knoll. They looked at one another sheepishly and began to laugh. Picking up Saihung's things, they started up the hill.

The island was smaller than a city block, and was studded with willows and pines. It had a commanding view of the lake shore, with several mountain ranges visible in the distance. The Grand Master and his acolytes had been exiled there by the government. No worshipers came. No students were there to learn. Just one old man and two elderly students.

Officially, the master was being protected from the turmoil of the new revolutionary society. It was rumored that Zhou Enlai himself had arranged this sanctuary, yet the refuge was also a prison. The Grand Master was too famous to be shot, but the government nevertheless wanted to ensure that he would not advocate religion to the masses. Although he was a renunciate, he was famous enough for them to fear his popularity. It was far better to isolate the older man in an unknown shrine.

The temple was the only building on the island, and was nestled atop a knoll. It faced south, the traditional orientation for most shrines. Much of it was in ruins or had been torn down. The remaining area was tiny, with only a main hall and a few smaller adjoining cells. Brick walls were plastered and whitewashed, the tile roofs were an ashen gray clay. The eaves had once been painted, though they were now bare and weathered, and moss and grass had begun to fill the crevices. Temples usually had a plaque at the lintel giving the name of the hall, but this one's was missing.

The acolytes showed Saihung through the open lattice-work doors. There was so much dust and earth worked into the grain that they might have been slabs of stone. The wood was cracked, as if vertical fault lines had shot through the mud-colored doors. There were no statues, no altar, not a single trapping of religion.

The Grand Master stood before the hall. He was at once familiar and yet, after Saihung's ten years in the United States, he seemed like an apparition. Saihung made his obeisance before his dark-robed teacher. He was emotional about seeing them like this, though he knew that they would not approve of his sentimentality. True to the doctrine of impermanence, utterly accepting of destiny, they seemed to be full of equanimity. Few words were exchanged, no excitement was expressed. For them, there was only the sense of their supreme control and harmony.

"You were kind to bring such generous gifts," murmured his master. He raised his disciple up.

Saihung had not thought that it would be such a thrill to hear his master's voice again. "I am honored to return," he replied softly.

"You can see that I have been reduced to rather poor circumstances."

"Your richness lies elsewhere, master."

"Obviously, it was not enough to save me nor those who stayed with me out of loyalty."

"You exaggerate," said Saihung. "We are your students for life."

"And what is this life but a dream?" whispered the Grand Master.

"Yes, and one that is over all too quickly," replied Saihung.

"That is why my only teaching to you is this: Understand impermanence. Contemplate the transitory."

The Grand Master gestured to the acolytes. "He has come a long distance. Let us sit down to a meal together."

They sat at an ancient wooden table in the middle of the dusty refectory. The acolytes busied themselves in cooking. By etiquette, it should have been Saihung's job as the youngest, but he was now the guest, and the Grand Master sat with him to talk. Saihung found his master's state of mind clear.

"Taoism cannot be practiced now. It cannot be used," said his master seriously. "Stay in the outer world, but keep Taoism alive and pure within you."

Saihung nodded in acknowledgment as he sat on the hard bench.

"Don't think that Taoism will save you," continued his master. "You have to save yourself. Taoism is a part of life, but life will not happen by itself. Each person has to go out and actively pursue life. In the same way, Taoism will not come to the passive person. Neither life nor realization comes without effort."

"It's a double effort, though," interjected Saihung. "I have to survive and I have to follow the Tao."

"In the past," responded his master, "time was slow. There was less pressure, less competition. But now, your life in the West is different. You must meet it head on, but you mustn't become involved with it inside. Tread the Way. Maintain and cultivate the five elements. Yield to the currents of life."

"It may be difficult to maintain balance." Saihung poured tea into his master's cup, grateful for the chance to listen.

"Not if you understand the difference between modern and ancient," replied the Grand Master. "The modern man does not know the unity of *yin* and *yang*. He wants only what is positive and pushes the negative aside. He doesn't realize that bad comes with good. In an effort to advance constantly, he turns to technology and accelerates his progress. Sadly, he does not realize that the greater his progress, the faster negative things will come. To the modernist, efficiency and practicality are paramount. Thus they are like beautiful oak trees, sturdy and strong. But oak trees are so valuable that they are cut down for boards."

"And the ancient way?"

"The mind of one who follows the ancients is like a gnarled tree. Ugly. No one wants it for wood, but it provides shade. It is both good and bad. Thus it survives, remains strong and self-sufficient."

"Constant striving only for positive results leads to destruction," reasoned Saihung.

"Exactly," said his teacher. "Modern man doesn't understand this. If Taoism is ever adopted by the modern West, it will mean the end of this philosophy. Taoism was developed in a particular place, and practiced by people who understand it. It goes very deep, has innumerable cultural roots. One would have had to be in China, living day by day, year by year, in order to be Taoist."

"Then Taoism will remain in China?" asked Saihung.

"No. It shall not even survive here. Chinese culture is now being Westernized and modernized. Modern architecture, medicine, and technology are all being eagerly adopted. Now there are radios, television, watches, cameras. Progress. Advancement. China is becoming more like the West, pushing only for the positive, ignoring the negative. China cannot absorb so much. There will be disease, illness, and mental imbalance. They have forsaken their native wisdom."

The acolytes came with the food. Saihung saw that the meal consisted almost entirely of things he had brought. There was the bread, fresh vegetables, various forms of bean curd. He wondered if this was out of politeness or necessity.

His master blessed the food, holding up the plates and offering it as if there were still gods to see it. They ate in silence and Saihung noticed that his master ate very little, as was his custom. Toward the end of the quiet meal, his master gestured with his chin as a way of urging Saihung to eat more.

"One cannot eat the way monks do while in the outside world," commented his master. "You must do what you can to sustain yourself. Society is not like a monastery. There is no shelter from the pressures and demands that will come your way. You must have fire and strength. Being Taoist does not mean passivity. It means that you meet life directly on every level demanded of you."

"What do you recommend?" asked Saihung. He tried to be gracious, but after such a long time, he did not need urging to fill himself up with the food of home.

"There are two rules to Taoist dietary practices: moderation and variety." The Grand Master observed Saihung's undiminished appetite. "First is moderation. Do not overeat, do not undereat. Do not go to extremes of fasting or overemphasis on any one food. Each meal should have moderate amounts of meat, vegetables, a starch, and a beverage. Avoid pork, duck, wild fowl, and shellfish, as we regard these to have toxins in them.

"Variety means that one eat according to the seasons. In winter, eat foods that will build the kidneys and the blood, such as lamb or veal. In summer, the cooling fruits, vegetables, and melons should predominate in your diet. Whatever the meal, try to have a minimum of three vegetables at every meal: one red, one green, one yellow. Do not have great amounts of single ingredients with your meal, but have a great variety of foods instead. If you follow the way of the ancients, you will have the strength to meet your challenges.

"Food is a primary source of energy. Thus it is foolish to restrict it. It is wisdom to control it, however, for this can be a significant factor in the cultivation of energy. One's *qi*, the very vital force of the body and soul, is formed from the essence gleaned from food. One might even go so far as to say that the foods you eat can be used to manipulate the consciousness."

Saihung marveled that his master would combine the most abstruse metaphysics with the most concrete of dietary recommendations. It was all part of the same subject to the master.

They were quiet again as the acolytes took away the dishes. Saihung insisted on helping. His master remained seated in the dining hall. As Saihung reentered the room, he looked at the man who had been his mentor for decades. The Grand Master had his back to him and sat upright on a bench. He was still, not meditating, but just sitting quietly. His thick white hair was gathered into a coil on his head and pinned. His dark robes made him seem almost formless. Saihung still considered himself a committed disciple. He even knew, but seldom wished to admit, that he would lay down his life for his master.

He wasn't supposed to have any emotions if he had truly realized the doctrine of impermanence and nonattachment. Such feelings came from the mind that he had been encouraged to still. If his current feelings meant that he had not reached a high level, then he accepted it for the time being. He saltily observed that even his master did not live without companionship, and that both he and his master still benefitted by the partly emotional ties that were between them. Ironically, his master and his lineage were his assurance of finding freedom from his inner turmoil. For the masters were like the chains that he had once used to climb Huashan's steep crevices: Link by link, they guided him through the dangers of life until he reached freedom. He had no doubt that he would be lost without that chain.

The acolytes came out, and Saihung observed them silently attend to the master. Again, he compared himself to them. They were what he could be if he only resolved his mystery. Or if he had been a much simpler man. Or if he did not have this mad combination of compassion and cruelty, sentiment and cunning, faith and cynicism. As he looked at Sound of Clear Water, the direct and honest carpenter, a man who worked with his hands, he realized that he might have been like him. Sound of Clear Water was a man of pure heart. Had Saihung stayed and become such a monk, he too might have found peace and tranquility. But he knew that he had been too complicated and ambitious a man. Sound of Clear Water, though a martial artist, was a more creative person.

Saihung compared himself to Mist Through a Grove. Clever at strategy, deeply intelligent, and a wonderful musician, he represented what Saihung believed that he himself could have been had he not had an ambitious side. Had life been different, Saihung might have sought a life as a painter or poet.

Saihung wondered whether there was some analogue to his own political manipulations, and was surprised when his eyes immediately focused on his master. Saihung flatly admitted to himself that the temples had been just as political and prone to the manipulations of power and position as the worst government assemblies that he had been to. At one time, even the Grand Master's own senior student had tried to usurp his master's position. Saihung knew that the Grand Master was quite capable of intrigue.

As he stood there watching the three men who had guided him since childhood, he understood himself a little better. He saw what he might have been like had his personality been balanced just a little differently. He was also reminded of the politics and intrigues, the drive for position and power that he might have dealt with had he stayed in the Taoist hierarchy. But whether for fate or his own stubborn will, he had gone a different path.

He refused to see that as something inferior to the way that his master and classmates had gone. He felt that he had gone through many of the same phases in life, exercised the same skills, faced the same pitfalls. The context was different, and that was all. Had he not fought on the streets of Pittsburgh, it would have been elsewhere, perhaps even against the soldiers who had invaded Huashan. Had he not involved himself with intrigue in government, then he would have striven for leadership within the temples. Had he not learned to find wonder and beauty wherever he traveled, then he would have learned it on the mountainside.

His master had sent him away to work out the same dilemmas that he would have had in the monastery. The only difference was that he was put in a wider field with more pitfalls and more bewildering choices to make. Saihung smiled to himself in resignation. Perhaps he should never have been named Kwan Saihung, which meant "Gateway to a Vast World." Perhaps the name would keep him a wanderer in search of his destiny. The hermit's ideal was to stay in one place and contemplate a universe that would reveal itself in the depths of meditation. Saihung's character meant that he would have to travel in the vast world to find his answers.

Saihung left that evening and returned a few days later with more supplies. He could only stay on the island for short times. They knew that the cadres were watching them constantly and they did not want to cause any suspicion.

Seeing the poverty that his master and classmates endured was heartrending to him, but he knew that his master would have it no other way. In a sense, the very humbleness of the island was perfect for the Grand Master. Only in plain circumstances could he continue to cultivate the Way. He and the acolytes truly seemed like fairytale people: the wise old man and his students. There were no such men in Beijing, and there were definitely no such men in the United States. Taoism, where antiquity coexisted with the contemporary, had now dwindled down to just this one tiny island.

"Master, let me stay with you," insisted Saihung impulsively when they met again. In the nights away from the island, he had begun to think two things. First that his master needed his service, and second that Saihung needed his master's discipline and instruction. No one recognized his need for a firm hand again more than Saihung himself. But the Grand Master again refused him.

"You cannot," said the Grand Master gently. "The government will never permit a young man like yourself to stay here. The acolytes and I are elderly; we are a threat to no one. But you are young: a potential subversive."

"I only want to come back."

"They'll know," said the Grand Master. "There are government observers everywhere."

"It's despicable."

"You still are very individualistic—and you've not lost your anger," observed his master. "China is not the place for you."

"America isn't either," replied Saihung. He thought about his circumstances in Pittsburgh. Humble surroundings were neither poetic nor spiritually rich there. He wanted the island.

The Grand Master strolled to the front of the temple. Saihung followed. Though physically large, Saihung was still a head shorter than the willowy sage. His master's robes trailed behind him as he walked with an ethereal grace. Saihung, in his everyday clothes, walked just on the ground. He was reminded of his boyhood days when he walked behind the old man, sneaking candy, disinterestedly meeting men of wisdom now vanished from the earth.

The sun came softly through the dusty and broken latticework. The paper windows had been patched repeatedly. In a corner, one of the acolytes had put some fresh patches up in a tentative attempt to improve the building.

The master pushed the doors open, and fresh air and light came in. A breeze came up and falling plum blossoms swirled lightly into the grey hall. They began to walk down to the shore. The gravel under their feet made a slight crunching sound.

"You are a man of many ambitions and of great energy," said his master. "You must exercise it and learn where it will lead you. You cannot yet practice complete emptiness. You cannot practice impermanence yet, for you have not yet had your fill of all that life has to offer. Go forth and strive mightily. When you learn the futility of your ways, you will find the key to your destiny. When you have fulfilled your destiny you will be satisfied. Once you are satisfied, your soul will rest. Only when you rest will you know stillness. In stillness is returning. Only in returning is there emptiness."

"Master, there is still so much for me to learn." Saihung came face to face with his master and made his appeal as sincerely as possible. "I am lacking. Please instruct me more."

"There is no time for that," said the Grand Master. He looked far to the distant horizon. There were diesel boats going across the water. "Your place is elsewhere, your destiny is beyond the borders of China."

"But Taoism is Chinese. How can I follow the Tao elsewhere?"

"You must solve that difficulty yourself. I can only give you one word of advice." He turned to Saihung and paused for a second before delivering the single word: "Persevere!"

Saihung looked up at his master. The eyes were clear, far seeing. The day made his hair and beard seem like strands of sunlight. He wondered how his master could deny him. Surely ten years in the West was enough. He hated the advice. The word for persevere also meant "bear it." He had the hideous image of working as a waiter for decades, all because of that one horrible word.

"Master . . ."

"Say no more," said his master as he gazed at a boat in the distance. "You have been away, but you have not determined your destiny. I told you long ago that I was awaiting your answer."

"But I've barely been able to survive."

"The answer!" demanded the Grand Master harshly.

"I—I don't have it."

The Grand Master turned from him. His face was strict, almost cold. "Then you should persevere."

The Grand Master looked up. "There is a boat nearby," he observed. "I think that we are being watched. You had better leave."

Saihung was reluctant. Of all the things he hated, he hated saying good-bye most of all. In the past, different masters had had to trick him into leaving when his period of living with them was over. One had even blessed Saihung in his sleep, for he was bound to leave once he had received a farewell benediction. As Saihung faced the Grand Master, he felt the same sadness of separation.

"Master," he said. "Come back with me. I'll work to support you."

"You need to support yourself," said his master. "I cannot leave China. My five organs are the five sacred mountains. The rivers are my blood, the air my breath. I could not reconstruct myself in a foreign land. Whatever my destiny holds, I must meet it on my native soil. Yours is different. You are destined to wander. I await you here, on this island. Now go."

"Master," said Saihung as he knelt down. He could see that there was no use in pleading any further. "Please take care of yourself."

His master said nothing. He waved his hand before Saihung in the gesture of blessing. The Grand Master looked for a few moments more at Saihung, then he turned back to his temple.

As Saihung traveled away from his master, the new civilization quickly presented itself. There were hundreds of distractions. Some were interesting, like new trucks, faces, attitudes. Some were annoying, like going through customs. Some were frightening, like being on his first airplane. By the time he was once again flying toward the United States, his master and the two acolytes seemed almost fictional. No one had the slightest knowledge that there was such a sage on an anonymous island. The government would cease to acknowledge them. The Taoists would never cooperate with the political world. They would become shunned, regarded as nonexistent.

The curious would never find them. Certainly, Saihung would never lead anyone to them, nor would the Taoists expose themselves. They liked anonymity. They did not like modernity and cared only for self-perfection. Showing themselves would only pollute them and lessen their chances for spiritual success.

He wondered what it would be like if he ever found the answer his master continually demanded of him. Perhaps he would finally gain an understanding of his master's wisdom. For centuries, Taoism was nurtured as a pure art. He considered himself lucky to have received some of it. He would not pass it on to the unworthy. If that meant he would never pass it on, he accepted it. Neither he nor his master would find that tragic. It was said only those who earned the opportunity from a previous lifetime would hear the Tao, and of those, only a minority would be worthy of receiving it. If he never found a way to perpetuate the system, he would let it die. That would be the way that he would cherish antiquity.

NINE

Golden Gloves

He returned to the United States with a feeling of loneliness. He found himself in a world where everything he most valued was now irrelevant. Maybe he needed a change. As much as he found comfort in Pittsburgh, he sensed that there was no future there. He'd try someplace else. He was getting older, and felt the need to make some more conservative decisions in his life. Having repaid his debt to Uncle William and Aunt Mabel, he wanted to establish financial independence. Saihung determined that he would save enough to return to a daily schedule of training and perhaps even found a school. That would take years of hard work and saving, but he felt ready to do it.

He went to New York to work for Uncle William's brother, a man he called Uncle Lenny. Uncle Lenny was a squat, balding man whose penchant for plaid shirts and worn, misbuttoned cardigan vests was an act of self-sabotage. He loved big cigars, shouting, and talking about his money and real estate holdings. His skin was spattered with dark spots and his shaving was usually uneven. In spite of all this, Uncle Lenny mustered enough charm to maintain a smart-looking, redheaded mistress.

Unlike his Pittsburgh sponsors, Uncle Lenny had no intrinsic affection for Saihung and he treated him like all the other employees. That meant that his work day ran for ten hours, his pay was fifteen dollars a day minus taxes, social security, and meals, lodging was a tabletop in the storeroom, and showers were a hose of cold water in the garage. Saihung read many books during that time, if for no other reason than they made a good pillow.

He tried his best to follow his master's advice, but how was he to blend with American culture? He decided the first thing he would do would be to improve his English. Reading was no problem—he had mastered that quickly enough—but speaking was another matter.

His solution was to go to movies every day off and reward his efforts with a cold milkshake. Some New York theaters showed as many as six movies for a dollar. He sat in the dark theaters, among the passed-out winos and necking couples, and studiously repeated the dialogue.

"My name is Bond. James Bond."

"Go for your guns, cowboy!"

"Th—th—that's all folks!"

His next effort was to discover how American society was structured. In China, he reasoned, there were definite differences between old and young. The Confucian order ordained a definite place for every person in society—father to son, husband to wife, children to elders. Old people wore dark black and blue. Young people wore bright colors. Old people were supposed to walk a certain way, young people were allowed to be carefree and energetic. But after much examination, he was astonished to conclude that there was no difference between young and old in America. It was not a stratified society when it came to formality and etiquette. There had been no American Confucius, and so there was no obvious structure for him to follow.

Seeing no way to integrate himself into society, he sought refuge in an institution more familiar. He began weight lifting and sparring at a gym on Canal Street. The building was on the northern side of the street that was the border between Little Italy and Chinatown. Though it was understood in those days that the two ethnic groups were unwelcome in each other's territories, Saihung was a Northern Chinese. His features were different from the Cantonese, who were more common in New York, and the ambiguity of his racial features was an asset.

The gym was on an upper floor. On the hot and muggy summer days, they left the windows open, and the traffic, honking, and shouting came up from the crowded streets. There were two small rings in the middle of the loft-like room. Many of the ropes and buckles were covered with black tape. These numerous layers of repair were common on the punching bags that hung from the ceiling, and the ubiquitous tape was even used to affix the posters of favorite boxers. Like images of patron saints, the faces and fists of such men as Joe Louis, Jack Dempsey, and Rocky Graziano overlooked the sweating, silent boxers.

He had been there a week, tentatively jabbing at the leather bags that were different than the ones he had worked with in China. No one was coaching him. He just imitated some of the moves that others did. A big heavyweight with a face like misshapen bread dough came up to him.

"What are you doing?" The man wore trunks with the name "Barry" sewn to them.

"Just fooling around," replied Saihung.

"Yeah, that's what it looks like." Barry looked down derisively. He outweighed Saihung by at least twenty-five pounds and was six inches taller. Saihung was irritated.

"What's it to you?" said Saihung rudely.

"I don't like you."

"So what? That makes two of us."

"Why don't you quit screwing around and step in the ring with a real man?"

Saihung assented without hesitation. Someone strapped big sixteen-ounce gloves and a headguard on him. Barry did the same. They climbed into the ring as the others in the gym gathered around to watch.

Barry came on savagely, catching Saihung in the face several times. Saihung didn't know what to do. He couldn't use any of his techniques with the big gloves on his fists, and he didn't know any of the footwork.

He tried desperately to fend off the incoming attacks, blocking the best that he could.

"Jesus! You move weird," said Barry. He caught Saihung with a good combination to the body and a heavy uppercut. Saihung backed up and Barry pushed him to the ropes.

Saihung tried to hit back, but his padded hands did not seem to have any effect on his opponent. Barry laughed at him and pounded him down to the canvas.

"Look, I don't know if you're a Spic, a Chink, or whatever," Barry said as he stood over the stunned Saihung. "But you should fucking get out of this gym. You're a bum!"

Saihung looked up at the puffy face, the flattened rectangular nose, the mop of black hair, the crooked blue eyes. He felt a raw hatred in him, but could not act upon it. Helplessly, he watched his tormentor leave the ring.

Everyone else went back to their activities without so much as helping him. As he sat up, he saw through his sweat-stung eyes a group of gray-haired men. Day and night, these old men sat in the gym like the retired masters that they were. These battered and scarred pugilists shared friendship and passion by living in the boxing world. With their cauliflower ears and broken noses, they were a grotesque lot. They had no pretensions; they had earned their positions. These veterans, who ranged in age from the fifties to the late sixties, never hesitated to enter the ring with arrogant men young enough to be their grandsons. More often than not, they brutalized the youngsters with their superior instincts and enormous fists.

Saihung went to them the next day to learn boxing. They were observant and wise when it came to the ring. They didn't care what words came out of a man's mouth, only how he moved, how powerful his body was, and how smart he was in the art of attacking and protecting. Saihung bribed them extravagantly with meals and liquor. This was the way he learned from the old men who watched, and talked, and spent every waking day studying the sweet science.

Saihung liked this study. He could throw himself into this training: roadwork, the heavy bag, the speed bag, conditioning with medicine balls, sparring, shadow boxing, calisthenics. But from those simple elements, an infinite world emerged. Boxing was at the very root of life whenever he was in the process of punching, aiming, looking, stalking. It was not a metaphor for life, nor was boxing merely an outlet for his frustrations or escape from his position in life. For Saihung, boxing was nothing more than itself: a pure act.

Violent, yes. But in the boxing world, the morality of violence was not what it was in the outside world. The abhorrence of violence was a manmade notion, without intrinsic divinity nor natural law. There was no judgment against violence in boxing. All that counted was moving, attacking, replying to the opposing movement. The fact that there was only one victor in a match did not invalidate the loser's action. Pain was not the same as it was for normal people, for whom it was to be avoided at all costs. For the boxer, pain was an acceptable part of his life. He was capable of going on in the face of excruciating agony, even of staying on his feet and punching while nearly unconscious. He inflicted violence, and his opponent inflicted it in return. No other connotations. No metaphors. No intellectualizing. Simple action with the brain and the body. Nothing else.

Boxing brought him to his absolute physical and emotional limits. Beyond the study, beyond the daily training, beyond the pursuit of the skill to fold an eighty-pound leather bag in half with the force of a single blow, was the thrill of the contest. No one was stupid enough to say if he would win or lose, not if he was honest with himself. He would only find out in combat, in testing, in answering the challenge with all the skill gleaned from the alchemy of talent and training. Each blow that he received to the head and the body weakened his conscious mind, pummeled his ego into silence. In a long match, there was only some unnamed other who fought in place of the one who occupied his body in everyday life.

That other was will. It was not the will to prevail over another man. It was the will to continue on in a ritual of supreme challenge. Only his belief in himself, his reliance on his knowledge, his powerful determination to keep on with somebody constantly battering at him and punishing his every second of carelessness could account for his survival in the ring and his fascination for fighting. His will was all that kept him from giving up, from obeying the instinct to flee from pain. It brought on another instinct: his will to exist.

Never in the ring, nor in the gym, did he ever question this will. But outside—away from the blood, and the sweat, the bitter cries with spit welling in the throat and hurt burning between the ribs—he sometimes questioned this powerful force that he relied upon to bring him through the rounds. It was precisely this will that barred his way to spiritual fulfillment. As long as he depended on this self, he could not realize its essential emptiness. At the same time, he knew that emptiness could not be realized without totally plumbing the depths of a self that was a phantom in ordinary circumstances. Fight on, he decided. He would not be able to transcend anything until he reached its limits. And boxing brought him brutally, harshly, and undeniably to his limits.

His coaches, an old Italian named Gus and a German named Alex, soon decided that Saihung was ready for the ring, and he began to fight in Golden Gloves matches. It was three simple rounds in front of crowds partisan to particular fighters or ethnic groups. No one ever came to watch Saihung fight. He was always a lone champion, an unknown whose name was applauded only accidentally or by drunks. Even that name was unreal. "No one is going to come see a Chinaman," Gus had said bluntly. "We'll put you down as Frank Kahn. Maybe at least the Irish will cheer you."

That didn't matter much to Saihung. He stood in the ring, nearly naked, his hands tightly wrapped, his fists bound in leather. He shifted his mouth guard impatiently as he eyed his opponent, a big Italian. They announced Frank Kahn. He turned a circle. There were apparently few Irish in the audience. They announced his opponent's name. There were cheers and screams. They went out for the referee's instruction, touched gloves, and retreated. Then the bell.

Saihung went out and immediately received several stinging lefts and a tentative right uppercut. He cursed. He could not kick, he could not use acrobatics. It was just him and his fists, just him standing on his feet upright. He counterattacked with several combinations. He felt the man's muscle through the gloves, felt the heat of his breath, heard his insults.

A blow got into his body and he felt his breath leave him for a moment. It hurt. The crowd cheered loudly. His anger welled up inside him. There was no need to hold back, no way to plan. There was only the consciousness of combat.

Saihung was a left-handed boxer. He threw two rights and then came in with a heavy left. His opponent covered up. Saihung went to the body, hooked into the kidneys. He heard a groan. He grunted in satisfaction and renewed his attack. But his next few blows were picked off on the man's gloves, and suddenly, his opponent bore in on him with a few quick jabs.

Saihung sidestepped and connected with a straight punch that sent a shower of sweat off into the dark room. It was not enough. There was a turn and the fighter bore down angrily.

The crowd screamed. There were insults, shouts of command from both corners. His two coaches were yelling at him, ordering him to renew the attack, telling him to use particular blows. He only shut them out. He had to concentrate. By the time he acknowledged their instructions and transmitted them to his hands, his opponent landed ten blows. There was no other choice but to rely on himself. He punched and dodged, hit back, tried to form some strategy. His breathing accelerated. He hit his opponent over and over, but the man still came, desperate and grim.

The round ended and he walked to his corner. They wiped his face, gave him water. Alex leaned over and uttered a string of obscenities in his heavy accent, mixed with his instructions. Saihung only nodded. He decided to use every bit of his knowledge.

The bell rang again and he went out, hands held high to guard his head. Boxers liked to go for the head. They figured that if they hit a man in the head long enough he would fall over. Saihung decided that his approach would be different, more systematic.

He faked high. His opponent's hands went up. Saihung came in with a devastating straight punch to the abdomen. He had folded a heavy bag. Now he folded the body over. He followed with two more punches and saw the man's heels come off the ground. He heard a familiar wheeze as the boxer struggled for breath, watched the blood rise to the face. The man was now not only fighting Saihung, he was fighting to keep control of his body. He had felt the pain, and that was nothing. But the lack of response, his inability to answer the call of the attack brought a desperate look to the man's face.

Saihung came with another series of combinations. He whipped the forearms away, exposed the heart, came in on his opponent's left side. Ribs were only a fragile cage to Saihung, and he hit them hard enough to jar the heart. The face reddened more, the eyes bulged. Saihung threw a stinging left above the nipple as the man tried to inhale. That interrupted his breath. A soft right set the head in position for the final knockout punch. He watched his victim fall heavily to the ring's floor.

"I don't know what the hell you're doing," commented Gus, "but it sure seemed to work." Saihung could only reply with an exhausted nod as he climbed from the ring. They took his gloves off and cut the bindings from his hands.

"Good work, man!" he heard as he walked to the showers.

"I lost money on you, asshole," he also heard. But he didn't care. At other times, he might have avenged such a remark. But he was too tired and had already satisfied his pugnacity in the ring.

He stood in the showers, the water stinging hot. He at least hoped that it would wash away the smell of the other man. Turning his face to the water, he let it run over his swollen eyes and down his neck before he picked up a piece of soap. He rubbed a few places where he knew there would be bruises the next day. It didn't matter to him. He knew how to take care of it. It was a part of boxing.

As Saihung stood in the shower, he felt good at having his first bout. He did not think to value one way of boxing over another. Learning to box was a part of his attempt to understand American life. He was a boxer, and it was essential to him that he knew how the people of the land fought. Western boxing had its good points and its drawbacks. It lacked the variety of Chinese martial arts and it was not as well integrated into the culture. But its training for pure punching power was undeniable, and much of boxing was, after all, predicated on the ability to hit hard and fast. In that there was no discussion of superiority of systems. All that mattered was how dedicated, disciplined, and talented a fighter was. Like Taoism, the crux of the matter always came down to the individual.

He marveled at the difference between a Western boxing match and a martial duel. Fights here were open to the public. Duels were not. The audience in New York consisted of teenagers and frustrated older adults. The audience in China consisted of all boxers. There, matches were on a simple platform with no ropes. Instructors sat on the main floor. Masters of schools sat on the first balcony. Grand masters sat on the highest level. The judges were the best in the martial world. These men, usually in their fifties, earned their office by fighting, not by democracy. They watched the match and decided the victor.

A referee was always present in the ring, and he had fthe right to intercede at any moment. Due to his expertise, he could usually anticipate a foul. Many was the time that Saihung saw a fighter stopped in mid-strike by some elderly referee. In at least one instance, the referee's grip had left a bruise where all the opponent's punches had not.

Victory was awarded after one man or woman conceded or fell (in the martial world, men and women dueled with each other on equal terms). There were no rounds, just continuous fighting. Unlike the bouts in the United States, there was no cheering, no lusty moving around. The masters watched in stillness and silence. The outcome was likewise received in silence. There was never applause, never any word of encouragement nor insult. Only quiet acknowledgment.

If there was any similarity at all, it was that both events seemed at once theatrical and ceremonial, though fighting was not sport, was not drama. It was the tableau of two people trying their might and their wills against one another. It was the reenactment of a fundamental and primal reality, the ritual of primitive consciousness on an altar of bone and sinew.

The more pugnacious Saihung became, the more restless he was in daily life. By the summer of 1964, he could no longer stand living in a storeroom eating mostly rice and a few vegetables and the scraps from Uncle Lenny's plate, which he always refused. He went to an employment agency and got a job as a cook at a restaurant in Queens; and at the same time, he moved in with a cousin at Eldridge and Broome Streets in the Bowery.

The building was a five-story brick tenement. There was a strange stoop with a Greco-Roman archway, and a battered steel door with one tiny window. Narrow stairs wound up from the ground floor and zig-zagged up to the roof. The walls were painted a dull flesh color, the doorways were dark brown. All the doors were solid metal. No matter what time of the day or night it was, there was never an open door nor anyone else in the dim hallways, only peeling paint and scurrying roaches. There was, however, plenty of noise. There were sounds of arguing, crying children, loud Latin music, people making love.

The apartment was one squat, four-square room with two windows and a blistered linoleum floor with a pattern like men's underwear. The brown and yellow wallpaper was torn in places, and underneath the plaster was cracking. The bathroom had seen its best days before Saihung had even been born. There was more black mold between the tiles than there was grout, and the faucets had been worn to the brass. The kitchen was a simple open place against the wall, just off the main door. There was a sink, a stove, a refrigerator. A single bare lightbulb hung down from the ceiling in the center of the room.

It was oppressively hot. Saihung tried to open the window. It would not budge.

"Don't open it," said his cousin, a young man named Wing. His name meant "Eternal Beauty," but Wing was as plain and thin as a stick.

"Why?"

"Because the Puerto Ricans and the Cubans will come in."

Saihung looked out the window. He saw the alleyway down below, where the tenants of the next building kept their garbage cans. Iron fire escapes were layered with years of paint and rust. The windows facing his had decorated arches that hinted at a time when landlords must have had more pride in their buildings. Most of the panes were dirty, scumbled with a layer of grime that obscured the small interiors. Some had potted plants; at a few windows, there was drying laundry. The setting light was orange through the chimneys and television antennas. The street dialogues were constant, punctuated with screams and shouts, curses and gunshots.

Saihung turned and looked around the room. There were five locks on the door and a special steel brace to wedge in the floor. There was little furniture: a table, some wooden chairs, several steamer trunks covered with clean but tattered towels. Wing pointed to some fold-up army cots. "This is all we have to sleep on. We put them away during the day."

He went to a trunk and pulled out a bar of steel a little over a foot long. "Take this with you whenever you go out. Wrap it in a newspaper. You will need it."

Saihung nodded as he took the cold blue metal in his hand. He had seen the street toughs eyeing him on the corner, the groups of noisy men playing dominoes in front of stores. Certainly, the sound of gunfire was even more alarming. He turned the weapon over in his hands. Survival mattered. Morality and ethics were for solitary philosophers. Living in America meant that he would have to deal with whatever was thrown at him. He did not think that the mystics of the sacred mountains nor the uptown intelligentsia would have done any differently if they wanted to survive.

"I'm going to work, now," said his cousin. "Our roommate doesn't get home until the morning."

Saihung watched him pick up a bag lunch and wrap his steel bar. His cousin walked out the door and reminded Saihung to lock it behind him immediately. This Saihung did, carefully wedging the brace in its brass socket.

He took off his shirt and changed into some shorts and

an undershirt. He was sweating so much that the cloth stuck all the more to his skin. Breathing was an unwelcome necessity. He went to the kitchen, washed a glass, and poured boiled water from the teakettle.

He sat down in the tiny kitchen. The floor sloped disconcertingly, and matchbooks and napkins were wedged under the legs of the table to make it level. A few dusty mousetraps lay sprung in the corners. He positioned a drab green electric fan in front of his face, but the propeller could do no more than to blow hot air in his face. Coming from a mountain temple, he was not unused to poverty-stricken conditions. But this slum was different. There was no charm, no rustic poetry in the simplicity of materials and the life free of material comforts.

He sat for many hours, just thinking of the future. He looked down at his hands, which had once been folded in contemplation beside mountain springs. The fingers, slender and tapered, had once caressed the strings of a lute. Now they were rough from the hot oil that splattered on them when he was cooking. The heat and the constant handling of four woks had put thick calluses on his palms. He had been trained to hold a writing brush, now he was always holding metal—if not the spatula in the kitchen, then the handrails on subway cars.

There was a chrome thermos bottle on the plastic laminate table, and he saw his reflection. He looked older. When he had seen himself on Huashan, his face had been fresh, young, hopeful. As he looked at himself in the polished silver, he saw the face of a man in his forties, features that were set, weary, a bit cynical. Though a stranger would not have placed him at more than half his age, he knew better. He saw every scar that he carried, noted the nearly invisible lines of disappointment.

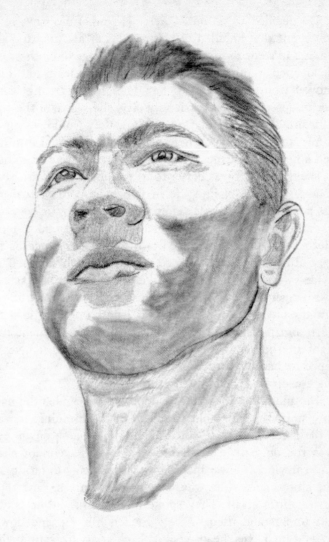

A self-portrait of Saihung.

He decided to go out. There was no use sitting in a tenement that smelled of baking plaster and melting asphalt. He went to his trunk to get a change of clothes. As he opened it, he saw a letter from Aunt Jean. She had moved from Pittsburgh to San Francisco. Writing wonderful descriptions of a friendly city, she wrote of the significant Chinese population and how they would welcome him. Saihung pondered her urgings, but he found in himself a new cautiousness. He couldn't even afford to go out to see the city. It was better to be patient, work hard, save money, and establish a life in which he could return to his spiritual aspirations. That was his goal.

Saihung moved some books aside and found a long cloth bundle. He unwrapped two long knives encased in special leather sheaths made to strap to his forearms. The blades were slightly curved, like the contours of a saber-tooth tiger's fangs. The metal was a flawless steel alloy, and the blood grooves that ran the length of the knife were deep and polished. Deeply etched ideograms caught the light in the slender brilliant strokes. It had been years since he had worn these, but if life was to be as rough as his cousin said, he wanted protection.

He undid the brace on the door and descended the narrow stairs. He went out the front of the building. It was a little cooler outside; the sun had long gone down. He was the only man on the street wearing a windbreaker and carrying a newspaper. The young Latins loitering on the stoops across the way were dressed only in tank tops or no shirts at all. They spoke in Spanish, and he could not understand them. A few looked him up and down with stoned eyes, heads cocked back at an arrogant angle, lips curled up, implied sneers. Their music was loud, blaring an insinuating beat of congas and trumpets. He glared back, never one to back down.

He looked up at the buildings around him. Old brick Victorian-era buildings were built tightly against one another. Their surfaces were etched by soot, rain, car exhaust. Cornices and archways were amazingly intact, considering the obvious age and decay of the buildings. The windows were opaque rectangles. At the roof line, he saw chimneys and water tanks, smokestacks, a jumble of rusted wire. The street was all blacks and ochres, red brick melting to dark grime, harsh yellow street lamps casting a lone spot per block. He walked north. The Chrysler building was a tiny tower, crowned with triangles that glowed in small points against the onyx sky. It was his only reminder that another world existed outside of the narrow street lined with cars and piles of garbage.

A block away from his apartment was a movie theater. For a dollar, one could see up to three movies. Saihung could not resist. He had always loved movies, and perhaps he could forget about his troubles for awhile and practice his English. He went in.

He found his way through by the flickering blue light from the movie screen. Half of the audience was asleep. Some were old men whose age or drinking had caught up with them. Others were passed out junkies who had sought a refuge in the dark, sweltering cavern. There were some families, and children ran screaming up and down the aisles, bumping him. He found a seat on the side section and sat down in a chair that sagged at the back.

He only saw horror movies that night. All he remembered after nearly seven hours were monsters trampling on Tokyo, creatures emerging from swamps, and aliens blasting people from office buildings. He did not learn much English, and there was mostly the sound of screaming and explosions. It was getting close to midnight and he had to go to work the next day. He went back into the night, and still the men were talking and laughing and watching him.

Even the next day, it still seemed dark whenever he was outdoors. He left for work before the sun came up, and it was night when he made his descent into the catacombs of the subway station in Queens. The tunnel was smoky and the air was thick with humidity. He was a man alone on the platform, waiting uncertainly for the next train to arrive. He spent long minutes staring down the straight corridor, counting the receding cadence of pillars, listening for the metallic sound of an approaching train.

He heard some laughter and some shouting. There was the sound of people jumping the turnstile. A group of young Cubans approached him.

He thought when the moment came that they would ask for money. They didn't. They were apparently only interested in the pleasure of beating him. Five of them surrounded him menacingly. One waved his hand provokingly in front of Saihung's face. There were urgings among themselves in their native tongue, but no one bothered to address the intended victim.

Saihung examined them quickly. He found them curiously short, but noticed that a few of them had weight lifter's bodies.

There was the click of a stiletto, and Saihung discarded the newspaper.

One man grabbed his hand and Saihung promptly brought the bar down and shattered his assailant's wrist. He spun around and caught another youth just above the ear. A blade cut toward him and Saihung dodged one of the heavy men attacking swiftly from behind. Swiveling away from this dangerous position, Saihung rushed furiously forward. He covered his assailant's whole face in the grip of his hand and squeezed hard enough to feel blood. Lunging forward, he pushed his struggling victim on to the tracks. As he put his foot back to the concrete, he rammed the end of the bar into the throat of the dagger-man. The man staggered forward and Saihung seized his wrist. A sharp twist dislodged the stiletto.

The biggest one tackled Saihung around the waist, but Saihung stood his ground. He did not let go of the knife-wielder's wrist, but brought the steel sharply down onto the head of the attacker. Blood wet his hand.

Only one man was left and, seizing him by the wrist and twisting, Saihung pulled him up. The man yelled loudly with the pain. Saihung put the bar against the elbow, and threw the man harshly to the ground with a mighty flip. A snapping kick broke his jaw.

They dragged themselves away. It was another twenty minutes before the gunmetal cars came down the track. Saihung gladly boarded and sat down in the loud and rocking car.

When he emerged from the subway station near his home, he was followed by a tall man. He might have to fight more. He walked swiftly up the street, stepping quickly over the few passed-out drunks that lay unmoving in his path. He had not settled down from the fury of fighting in the station, but he did not want to fight again. He was afraid that he would not remember to hold back. These were not desperate people who needed something to eat. These were men who got their enjoyment by sadistically hurting people.

He turned the corner on to Eldridge, and stopped. An enormous dark man stood in his way. He was wearing a blue short-sleeved shirt with tropical colors. His ebony skin glistened with perspiration, and his crooked teeth were stained and brown. Saihung turned. The shadow he had picked up at the subway station was right there. Saihung saw the flash of brass on the fist that came out of a pocket. There was not even the chatter of Spanish as there had been earlier, only the menacing closing of the trap.

Saihung lashed out with the bar, but the shadow grabbed it. He loomed over Saihung and shot his hand out for his jaw. Saihung intercepted it, grabbing a finger and bending it back. He twisted the arm in its socket, and hit the man on the front of the rotated shoulder, dislocating the joint.

Saihung heard a sound, and cocked his head in time to avoid a heavy blow. But though he protected his head, the iron links struck him full on the back. He turned and ducked the backhand return of the chain. Saihung whirled in close and hit the man hard enough to send blood and teeth into the gutter.

They staggered angrily toward him. He backed up a few paces. With a great deal of swearing, they made a few lunges that he sidestepped. Finally, it seemed as if he had no other choice. With his back to the door of his apartment building, he pulled out one of his own daggers. The crescent of steel was almost incandescent in the night. The men paused.

"Come on! come on!" shouted Saihung. "I'll give it to you right here!"

They turned and fled. Saihung unlocked the door and rushed in. He checked under the stairs for anyone hiding there, and ran up the stairs to his room. There was no one else inside. It was oppressively hot. He looked out the dirty windows. They remained closed.

There was a park on the southern edge of Chinatown. Saihung had acquired the habit of going there since he first arrived in New York, and he still went there in the early morning to work out. He came in darkness and usually left before the sun came up. A romanesque granite building that looked like a cross between a dance-hall and a grandstand bordered the park, and Saihung fancied it to be like the pavilions in China.

Other men came to work out in the park as well. They practiced different forms that they favored, manipulated staffs and swords for the exercise. Some even knew *qigong*, and Saihung could see their solitary figures doing deep breathing or standing in contemplative postures.

It was hot in August. Even the dark summer mornings seemed warm on his skin. He stood in the black shadow cast by the pavilion's upper level and made himself absolutely still. He thought of his *dan tian*, a spot of concentration in his lower abdomen. According to the classics of Tai Chi, this was the moment analogous to the void that preceded the universe. It was *wu wei*, nothingness. He held no thoughts.

The first moment of the universe, when time and energy and matter were all set into motion, was believed to have been triggered by thought. In the same way, he decided to begin. This was volition. There could be no movement without it. He inhaled, and the breath stirred the repository of energy in his *dan tian*, just as the first ray of thought that flashed through the void had generated breath.

His arms began to rise. The energy rushed up his back and out to his hands with a tingling sensation. His fingers began to fill with blood. Breath and blood and consciousness all flowed from his center out, as the universe had first expanded from a single point of infinity. He lowered his arms, bent his knees, and the energy sank back to his *dan tian*, descended to the bottom of his feet. He had established upper and lower, rising and falling, expansion and return. In the movement of two arms, he had distinguished *yin* from *yang*. All this occurred in the first movement of Tai Chi Chuan. By its very structure, it reflected the very beginning of the universe. It did not need discourse nor philosophical speculation, it taught by doing. It taught on a level that the conscious mind did not acknowledge.

He began to move his arms and take a variety of stances. Outwardly, the postures seemed similar to other styles of martial arts. After all, the science of footwork and strikes was already well established before Tai Chi had ever been created. It was a relatively young martial art, which had reached the zenith of its forms only within the last one hundred years; it was natural that it should resemble other styles. But inwardly, it was much different.

Other styles had features that were outwardly apparent. This was part of the reason that a fighter like Saihung could observe the patterns of a style and adapt even during the heat of battle. Tai Chi, however, could only be appreciated by the person doing it. So much of its qualities lay within the mysterious arrangement of its movements, the slowness that encouraged healthy circulation, the deep breathing that became automatic when the postures were done correctly. What was hidden in Tai Chi was the secret that only the practitioners knew: Energy could be circulated in a special way if one took the trouble to keep certain alignments of the body.

These alignments were a straight back, rounded shoulders, pelvis tilted upward, head straight, feet firmly planted, and body relaxed. This simple set of concordances set the gates of the body open; and if one had not clogged the pathways of the body by poor diet or indiscreet living, the energy would spontaneously move on its own. The first thought in the first posture set it into motion. Throughout the rest of the movements, it would flow on its own. No ordinary person could see this on the outside, but inside, the practitioner could feel the movement and enjoy the sensation of life-force itself. By relaxing and letting go, he gained everything. He loved feeling the movement deep beneath his skin.

Something definitely animated the body. The most detailed investigations into biology, chemistry, and matter would never account for the mystery that was life. But here in the process of Tai Chi was the sensation of life itself. It was not just blood flow. It was not just the simple tingling of nerves. It was the unmistakable feeling that a force was flowing like a tide throughout the body. Not only did this force leave one feeling fresh, alert, and renewed, but it also responded to consciousness.

The quality that made him a living human being was not simple energy like electricity from a socket. It was something more subtle, more complex. It would respond to his thoughts, and it could be disrupted by his thoughts. That was why there was meditation. The more focused one's thinking was, the more one could direct and learn from the forces within.

When the energy flowed, the channels were purified, the organs were regulated, and the subtle channels of the nervous system were cleansed. Consciousness had set the universe in motion. The motion in Tai Chi did the opposite. It could affect the consciousness of the individual. Both sides of the body were moving, the eyes were following the hands, the spine was continuously being rotated and stimulated, and it was inevitable that both sides of the brain would be opened at the same time. All of this happened through the gentle movements of a set of over one hundred postures.

There were things that Tai Chi could not do, of course, and that was why neither a martial artist nor a spiritual person could rely wholly on it as a form of exercise. While it was excellent at circulating energy, it was not very good at increasing or cultivating it in the first place. This function was reserved for other procedures such as *qigong*, various calisthenics, and even herbs. It was also inadequate to build muscle strength. And it could never succeed in reaching the level of spiritual insight that meditation did. But for its genius of internal cultivation, its celebration of the body as a microcosm of the outer world, and its contemplative movement, it was unique among all the exercises.

He practiced other martial arts, reviewed the weapon techniques that he relied upon to save his life in his neighborhood. He went to the park every day to stand in the quiet time before there was even morning light. At work, he was someone to be ordered around, a body to cook meals for the sake of business. In the ring, he was a fighter against a man whose face was often obscured by a headguard. In the streets, he was the target of men whose language he did not learn. Only there in the anonymous dark did he feel that which was within him.

Two years after he had begun boxing, Barry, the fighter who had beaten Saihung in the gym, appeared again. Once more, he watched Saihung at the bags, asked who he was. He had forgotten Saihung, but Saihung had not forgotten him. He watched the man with the bloated face walk toward him.

"What are you doing?" Barry asked him aggressively.

"Just fooling around," replied Saihung noncommittally. He wondered if this was a rehearsed routine with Barry.

"Yeah, that's what it looks like."

Saihung decided to cut the ritual short. "I don't like you. Step in the ring or get out of my face."

"Asshole!" Barry leaned over Saihung menacingly. "I'm gonna make you ugly!"

Saihung looked over at Gus. The grizzled senior coach nodded his approval.

"All right," shouted Saihung. "We'll see whose face looks uglier when this is over. I want four-ounce gloves!"

Barry knew what that meant. Four-ounce gloves had no padding at all. He hesitated a moment, but his pride was too strong. "OK, chump. It's your funeral."

"You bastard!" Saihung's face turned crimson with fury. "I'm going to piss on your grave!"

Saihung went over to Gus, who taped his hands, slipped on the gloves, and put a headguard on him.

"I know you're mad," said Gus, as he made sure that everything was cinched up. "But you keep your head out there, OK?"

Saihung said nothing in response. He nodded. He never took his eyes off the pale-skinned Barry. Gus pulled one of the ropes down and pushed Saihung gently into the ring.

Barry looked at him eagerly. Saihung could see that his reach and weight gave him confidence. Barry grinned maniacally.

The bell rang and the other men began to cheer. The first time they had fought, men had watched silently; no one knew Saihung. But this time he had acquaintances who shouted their encouragement. Barry charged at him with a barrage of heavy blows. Unwarily, he threw his might into the first skirmish without any tentative punches. Saihung counterpunched, and stung some hard jabs to Barry's arms. The punches hurt enough for Barry's guard to falter. Saihung noted with pleasure the sudden look of bewilderment on Barry's face. Two years of hitting the heavy bag had given Saihung's punches a new authority.

Barry tried to punch Saihung toward the ropes, but Saihung moved to the side and hit Barry's face several times. He saw a swelling. Barry came in again, tried to maul Saihung, and Saihung punished the move with heavy hooks that caught the side of the face. He followed with a straight overhand that pushed Barry's jaw far to the side.

By the second round, Barry circled Saihung a little more carefully. Saihung took some hard lefts, but then opened up several cuts on Barry's face. Blood began to smear on the front of Saihung's gloves as he threw punch after punch. He felt the heavy impact of his knuckles on bare skin and bone. People began to yell from the sidelines, and Barry began to curse loudly as he came in with a heavy uppercut that nearly knocked the wind from Saihung's lungs.

Saihung pushed him off, and looked at Barry angrily. Saihung was aware that he had lost his own temper, that he was a raging boxer. He swept aside his reservations, and for a few exchanges, he and Barry stood toe to toe slugging it out. Saihung hit him with a right, made sure Barry was looking, and then dropped the guard of his own left hand while feinting again with his right. Barry took the bait and threw a crushing right hand which Saihung dodged. Before Barry could withdraw the hand, Saihung stepped inside and came up with the hardest left he could muster. Barry went down, his jaw and nose nearly bent out of human proportions.

Saihung stood over the fallen man without grace or composure. He shouted obscenities, spat on his face. "Now who's uglier?" he demanded of the bloody and immobile face. Gus rushed up to drag him away. The ring filled with men.

"You're getting a little crazy," Gus whispered. Saihung said something obscene in response. Gus shrugged. "Hey. I'll talk to you when you've cooled down."

It was not until hours later, sitting alone in the light of the lone incandescent bulb that hung above his locker that Saihung began to reflect on the fight and Gus's pronouncement. It was the first time that he considered whether he had gone too far from his path.

Saihung corresponded regularly with his aunt and uncle in Pittsburgh. Toward the end of 1968, they wrote that their house had been bought by the city. The site had been part of land designated for a freeway. They had no choice but to move.

Aunt Mabel and Aunt Jean, who had once worked in the same laundry, had been corresponding. Aunt Mabel wanted to move to San Francisco, or at least any place that did not aggravate her arthritis as the winters in Pittsburgh did. Surprisingly, Uncle William did not want to move from the city. He had lived there for forty years and had grown quite attached to it.

Uncle William feared old age. His letters constantly appealed to Saihung to return to take care of the elderly couple. Saihung did not object to helping them, but he did not want to move back. He, too, thought seriously of San Francisco. He could not continue forever with his New York life. He was getting varicose veins from all the standing that he had to do as a cook, he was never sure if one of the street toughs would get lucky with a pipe or zip gun, and he had been wondering about his emerging savagery.

His final matches as a Golden Gloves boxer were fought in Madison Square Garden, which represented the achievement of a certain plateau to him. But as he sat in the dressing room after a fight that he had won by knockout, he accepted the fact that he had changed. He was off course. He had boxed enough to be able to decide when to knock a man out. He had begun to enjoy the sound of ribs breaking. There was such a thing as a killer instinct, and his own rose up in him with increasing vehemence. With some fright, he saw that the eagerness for triumph had obscured all his other priorities.

Gus came into the room.

"Hey, Frankie Kahn!" exclaimed Gus. "You were great out there! Did you ever think of turning pro?"

"No," replied Saihung before he could consider what he was saying. "I'm quitting."

"What the hell do you think you're talking about? You don't quit like that!"

"I do what I want!"

"Hey! Cool down! It's an old problem. I've seen lots of fighters go through what you're going through. It's a postfight letdown. Give it a rest for a couple days. You'll come around. And when you do, son, there are some people interested in you."

"I'm going to hit the showers. I'll think it over."

"Sure, sure," said Gus. "You'll come back."

"Yeah," said Saihung off-handedly. But he knew that he would only go back to clean out his locker.

That night, he walked to the waterfront. He pulled out his daggers. Though he had never used them, he had threatened plenty of people with them. He entertained the suspicion that the daggers themselves, through some unknown force, attracted evil to him. Superstitiously, he felt that a weapon always demanded to be used. By carrying them, he was inviting trouble.

Boxing and street fighting differed from the ideals of martial art. Both were considerably more primitive, not in technique, but in meaning. The martial principles that he had been raised with emphasized virtue, chivalry, and honor. Only two people who were on the same level dueled. Sometimes they only fought for respect. Defeat came to all fighters. No matter how great, every one had felt what it was to lose. Perhaps a fighter even answered a challenge knowing that he was the inferior one. But in the martial world, it was good enough that one was valiant. Losing did not necessarily compromise one's honor.

Saihung felt that there was no honor in the fighting he had done. He did not honor his opponents, and they did not respect him. That was not the type of fighting that he had trained for decades to do. Martial arts was for discipline and dignity, not for sweating and shouting and bloodying and slaughtering.

He turned the blades over. Their curve echoed the crescent moon. He held them up one last time, remembered how he had had them custom made of the finest metal available, how he had consecrated them with the appropriate runes and mantras. Weapons had power. Weapons had spirits. But power and other spirits could possess a man. He wanted to stop fighting. He already had tickets away from New York. Saihung flung the daggers as far as he could into the river.

Gate of Liberation

Saihung, Aunt Mabel, and Uncle William took the train out to San Francisco. Movers would ship most of their possessions after they had established themselves. This was done easily with the aid of Aunt Jean, the pleasant middle-aged friend they had known from their Pittsburgh days. His aunt and uncle moved to a small apartment on the eastern slope of Nob Hill. Saihung found a single room on Stockton Street above a butcher shop.

His first days in the often foggy San Francisco were unusually sunny and warm. He happily walked street after street in exploration of his new home. He walked from Chinatown through North Beach and then began to climb steep steps on the sidewalk toward Coit Tower. The surrounding bay made the city seem especially tranquil to him. As he first climbed Telegraph Hill, and then Russian Hill, he could always see the serene blue of the distant bay, placid and wide. He felt welcome.

The people seemed friendlier, open, and more relaxed than those whom he had met in Pennsylvania and New York. Though he soon discovered that there was racial tension even here, it was not so immediate nor so savage as what he had experienced before. Perhaps it was because the city was simply not so densely populated. As he walked up to the crest of Hyde Street and looked down a steep hill to the piers at the bottom, he met very few people. Compared to China, where sidewalk traffic was like a major parade, or New York, where people were on the streets at any hour, San Francisco seemed almost tiny and intimate.

He wandered into a park past some tennis courts and then down several flights of concrete stairs. He could see hill upon hill, and beyond the waters even more hills, like the spine of a dragon lying on the horizon. He walked by some recently painted green park benches where a few people sat casually reading the Sunday paper. Strolling to a lower level, he found an empty bench with a view of the Golden Gate Bridge and sat down.

There was just a hint of salt in the air, mixed with traces of pine trees. The vista was high, and he was able to see the Marin headlands, the straits leading to the Pacific Ocean, the almost indistinguishable squares of houses on the slopes to the north. Not since he had been on Huashan had he had the opportunity to feel that he was standing on a high vantage point. It felt good. It made his recent past seem all the farther away.

He sat there contentedly for a long time until he realized that he was due at a welcoming banquet. Saihung walked back over the hill and down Jackson Street to his aunt and uncle's apartment. He rang the bell and smiled when his aunt came out in a blue coat and a hat with a veil.

"Auntie," said Saihung. "It's quite warm outside."

"Wait until you're seventy," laughed his aunt. "You'll wear a coat too."

She walked slowly down the stairs. Saihung noticed that she seemed a little more stooped, a little tinier.

Uncle William locked the door behind him. He was wearing a brown striped suit and a camel-colored hat.

"Ah, Ox Boy! It's good of you to come escort two old people."

"It's not natural for young people to be with old," commented Aunt Mabel.

"Yes," agreed Uncle William. "We aren't too slow for you, are we?"

"I don't mind," responded Saihung. "We're all new to this city. Why not stick together? We are practically relatives."

"You're kind to pretend," said his aunt.

"Are you finding it easy to get settled?" asked Saihung.

"I'm making many new friends. Jean is showing me the city, and I've met some of her coworkers. You uncle has been down to the family association quite a bit."

"So you like it here after all?" Saihung asked as he turned to his uncle.

"It will do," said Uncle William gruffly. "But I miss my Buick."

"Oh, forget that thing," said his wife scornfully. "Both you and it were getting too old to drive around together anyway."

"And ice cream," continued Uncle William, studiously ignoring his wife. "There don't seem to be many ice cream places here."

"I'm sure there are a few," said Saihung.

"Where?" demanded his uncle.

"I don't know . . . I'm sure we could find one."

"Yes," said his uncle emphatically. "It should be done before the next Sunday."

"Stop ordering him around," said Aunt Mabel. "Ox Boy has his own life to live. Besides, how can you talk about ice cream when you have a whole banquet ahead of you?"

Uncle William shook his head. He leaned over to Saihung.

"I envy you," he whispered. "You were smart not to get married."

"I heard you!" said Aunt Mabel in a tone of mock outrage. Uncle William began to laugh, and his wife was soon laughing at his teasing too.

The banquet turned out to be a rather modest affair. There was roast duck, a whole steamed rock cod, beef with broccoli, sea cucumbers. Aunt Jean sat across from Saihung. She was a short, plump woman in her fifties. Her skin was wrinkled at her forehead and mouth. Her eyes were narrow and closely set, so that she seemed slightly cross-eyed, even when she was looking far away. She dyed her hair jet black and it was always coiffed into a virtual helmet. Gaudy gold and jade bracelets dangled on her wrists. Though she wore a *cheongsam*, the traditional Chinese high-collared silk gown, she had an old cardigan thrown over it. Comfort was what was important, she reminded Saihung.

Her husband, Henry Chan, was a large man with a brown and sagging face. He had large puffy bags under his down-sloping eyes, and thick lips that usually were wrapped around enormous cigars. A full bottle of brandy sat before him, and the only thing he drank it with was a glass. He never laughed, though his idea of dinner conversation was to make fun of other people under the pretense of good humor. He enjoyed blowing smoke magnificently over the table.

"Hey!" he shouted to Saihung. That was Henry's typical form of address.

Saihung looked over.

"How you like it here?" Uncle Henry did not speak much Chinese. His English, on the other hand, was outrageously accented. Saihung wondered just which language his uncle was comfortable with.

"I like it fine," said Saihung, straining to be polite as more cigar smoke came his way.

"Hey! Your Aunt Jean went through a lot of trouble to get you here." He stubbed his cigar into a glass ashtray.

"Yes, I know. We all appreciate it."

"OK. Hey! Eat more. This food's expensive, you know." Henry gestured expansively over the table and looked at Saihung with red-rimmed eyes.

Saihung held his temper. His uncle's comment certainly did not stimulate his appetite.

"You know how I can afford to do this?" Uncle Henry continued without any encouragement. "I worked hard. Saved my money. Invested it. Chrissakes, look at you. It's time that you did something too. Don't just throw your money away on women."

Saihung did not know what to say.

"Hey, I know. Young guy. They all do it. But if you want to get ahead, you save. Got anything?" Henry was waving his hands at Saihung. A large, gaudy jade ring gleamed on his little finger.

"Yes, I do," said Saihung with as much dignity as possible.

"Put it in the bank over on Grant and Jackson. Best interest rates." He turned to look into his glass of whisky.

Saihung said nothing. Henry looked up suddenly, his droopy eyes opening in surprise.

"Chrissakes!" he exclaimed. "Don't tell me that you stuck it all in a mattress somewhere?"

No, he hadn't. He carried it with him. He did not trust banks.

His uncle spoke Chinese for the first time. "You stupid country bumpkin! Don't be dumb. You never heard of interest?"

Of course Saihung had heard. But he wasn't sure how finances worked in the United States. His embarrassment prevented him from responding.

"You want to make your money grow, you invest it," explained his uncle. "Take me, for example. I got a nice deal coming up to open a big restaurant. All the investors are getting together and we'll make a nice profit. Hey, you could do it too."

"I don't know that end of the business," said Saihung.

"That's the beauty of it. You get the experience of others to work for you. Think it over. Get a deal going like that."

"Henry," interrupted Aunt Jean. "Stop talking about money all the time. Ox Boy doesn't want to listen to all your bluster."

They finished the last course of the dinner, and Saihung was thankful that his two uncles found enough in common for him to be left out of the conversation. Eventually, Uncle Henry stood up unsteadily. Saihung was afraid that his uncle would pass out, but the man was determined. "Hey! You enjoy yourselves. I'm going to the bar!"

Saihung went the next day to a Chinatown employment agency and applied for a variety of jobs. He found that there were still few positions available to Chinese: cook, waiter, laundry, houseboy. He wanted to stick to restaurant work; that was what he knew best. The first job he got was as an ice cream scooper across from the topless bars on Broadway. It took several months of applying before he got a better position as a waiter at a downtown men's club. It was back to eight hours a day, but at least he was away from the Chinese employers who paid little for long hours. He continued to save and added that to the money that he had brought with him from the

East Coast. Within a year of his arrival in San Francisco, he had put together a sizable sum of money, enough to have bought an entire house for cash. But he did not want a house. He wanted enough money so that he could live independently, perhaps still persuade his master to come live with him. He remembered Uncle Henry.

"How did that restaurant do?" asked Saihung when he met his uncle on the street.

"Fine," said Henry. "We sold it already." He lit up the stump of the cigar he was carrying.

"So fast?"

"Hey! There were three partners. We each made thirty thousand." He blew cigar smoke out of his mouth and watched it drift down Stockton Street.

"I've got money to invest," said Saihung in a quiet voice.

"How much?" His uncle did not even turn to look at him.

"As much as what you made on the restaurant."

"You should buy a house. Get married," advised his uncle.

"I'd rather invest it."

"With me? Forget it. I don't do business with relatives." He looked with a bored expression at the glowing end of his cigar.

"But I don't know who to trust."

"Well, maybe," said his uncle noncommittally. "I'll call you if another deal goes through. You need people who can handle everything. Do you know how to get permits? Do you know the guys in City Hall? It takes a lot of wheelin' and dealin'."

Saihung knew nothing about such things. That was why he needed help. "You'll call me?"

"Yeah. Don't Jean have your number?"

Saihung nodded. Eventually, Uncle Henry helped him invest in a restaurant.

Uncle William died two years after they moved to San Francisco. Saihung did his best to comfort Aunt Mabel and personally arranged for his uncle's burial. A year after, Saihung came back to his hotel room and found a message that his aunt was ill. Alarmed, he walked immediately to the community hospital.

The interior was dark, a narrow hall lit in sepia tones. A rubbery faced nurse with a double-pointed white hat looked at him indifferently. "No visitors!" she said curtly.

"It's not ten o'clock yet," replied Saihung patiently. "And I am a relative."

"So what?"

Saihung moved forward threateningly. "So I want to see her. Now!"

She jumped a little. "Name?" she said, a little more meekly.

"Mabel Yee."

"Room 402. You've got five minutes."

He walked by her station without saying anything more and raced up the stairs. The wooden steps creaked with each step. The air was very warm, and smelled of camphor and alcohol.

The doors to the individual rooms were painted with a heavy red paint. There were wooden bins on the doors for charts. Some overstuffed chairs were in the hallways, as if to provide places for convalescing patients to rest as they tried to walk. The corridor was dim, the lightbulb hanging from the ceiling was bare. He found his aunt's room and went in to find a man dressed in black standing over her.

"Who the hell are you?" demanded Saihung protectively.

The gray haired man turned around. He was tall, ruddy faced, blue-eyed. Saihung saw the white collar around his neck. The priest was holding a rosary and a Bible.

"I came to help your aunt."

"Ox Boy . . ." whispered his aunt weakly. "Make him go away."

"She doesn't want you here," declared Saihung. "Please leave."

"I understand that you might be upset at this moment. But it is often a comfort to hear the word of God."

Saihung restrained himself from being rude. "My aunt has her own religious beliefs."

"There is only one God."

"I'm not in the mood," said Saihung, grabbing the priest by the arm. He shoved the man out the door and closed it firmly.

He pulled the curtain across the room and sat down beside his aunt. She was elevated in an overstuffed hospital bed. Dressed in a pale gown, she lay small and still under the stiff white sheets. A lamp cast yellow light low on the bed. Some flowers in an old porcelain vase had already begun to wilt in the heat. The dark window was like a sheet of slate. Saihung saw his aunt's white reflection. She might already have been a ghost.

Her hair was laid out around her head in small waves of silver. Aunt Mabel's face seemed to be more wrinkled, the eyes like jewels sunken almost entirely into the mass of her pale flesh. Her lips were dry, colorless.

"Where does the soul go?" she asked with childlike directness.

Saihung did not even think to engage in scholarly discourse. "It will be a comfort. The gods will take you. You will be reborn."

"Heaven is hard to imagine," she murmured. "It's harder to imagine than remembering China."

"Auntie, don't talk if it makes you tired."

"I've laid here all day. I want to talk. All I've thought about is my home in the village that I haven't seen for fifty years. How odd to think of it so vividly. Do you think my soul will go back there?"

"If you so will it."

"Ah, yes . . . if I so will it."

A voice came from the hallway. "All visitors must leave!"

"I must go, Auntie," said Saihung softly. "I will come in the morning."

"Yes, come," replied his aunt. "Read me the sutras, so that I may find my way to the next world."

"I will be here," he promised as he adjusted the sheets.

As he walked into the foggy streets, he wondered about what he had so easily told his aunt. Aside from what was written in scriptures, there was no guarantee that the gods existed or that there was even such a thing as reincarnation. But he did believe that the soul could go where it wanted to go upon death. He had enough respect for the human mind to understand that it could transcend death.

If Aunt Mabel was determined enough, she would indeed go back to her village. If her prayers were fervent enough she could be led to paradise itself. It was all the mind, with its different characteristics. The mind that was the intellect, that classified, reasoned, and made decisions; that doubted; that was memory. The mind that was self-belief, a will to exist. The mind that was silent observer.

Did his aunt exist? Of course his master would say no. But what he meant was that his aunt did not exist separately from Saihung. That what divided them from one another was merely a misconception, a little confusion. That made his aunt's impending death all the more profound to him. He was dying too.

He found sutra books, went to her side the next day. But she was unable to hear him. He sat there for a long time praying, the first that he had really prayed since he had left the temple. He had been taught from childhood that the chants of the devout could lead the soul of the dying, guide them at the moment when they were most bewildered. He whispered his prayers sincerely over and over, determined to escort his aunt to the other side. She never awoke to see him again.

Only at sporadic moments did he see the sheets rise and fall with slight breathing. Breath was the very basis of life, but breath was slowly abandoning her. There was neither enough going in, nor even enough energy to take the air. His aunt could no longer seize life, for the only way anyone stayed alive was by constantly harvesting the breath around them. Life was leaving Aunt Mabel. She could no longer hold on to it.

Saihung looked down at her hands, shriveled and gnarled roots lying on the clean white fabric. Twisted, curled, they had been painfully distorted for years by arthritis. She had been unable to straighten, in spite of medication and Saihung's massaging. Her profession had crippled her permanently. But as he looked at her spotted brown hands, he remembered the care that she had taken in making dim sum, the patience with which she used to mend his clothes.

He prayed there the whole day, determined that he would do whatever he could to lead her soul safely into death. With single-minded concentration, he repeated the chants, sent his most heartfelt feelings. Destiny could not be stopped, but at least he would do whatever he could to ease its final path.

Aunt Mabel died the next day in her sleep. Aunt Jean and Uncle Henry were there, and helped ease him through the confusion of all the arrangements. There were many old women at the funeral, friends that his aunt had made in San Francisco, and young people who had escorted the elderly. They buried her next to her husband, on a grass knoll overlooking the bay. Incense was burning, candles flamed brightly over the grave, flags with holy words fluttered in the wind. Taoist priests chanted and prayed for her soul.

He looked down as a young man shoveled earth over the coffin. Where was Aunt Mabel? For all his training and his meditation, he could not see where she had gone. Uncle Henry laid a comforting hand on Saihung's shoulder.

"Don't take it too hard, son," he said in his rasping voice. "She is in a much better world."

Saihung looked up quietly. He thought that it was an idiotic thing to say. But he only nodded.

"Hey. Come by and see me and Jean when the mourning period is over, OK? It might be time to celebrate the restaurant."

"It's not respectful to talk about it now," said Saihung.

"Don't take it wrong. I only mean that it's too bad Mabel won't see it." Uncle Henry rolled his eyes. He was unfamiliar with devoutness.

"I will come in a month," said Saihung.

"All right. You watch out for yourself until then."

When Saihung returned to his room, he sat down on the edge of his bed and thought about his aunt. It would be wonderful if he could see her, if he could somehow know that she was all right. As he meditated, he could not detect any presence of Aunt Mabel. She was gone. The masters would simply have told him that she never existed. They would have told him that she had merely existed in his mind. That she came to be something meaningful to him because of his own mental weakness.

In China, he would have found a sorcerer and paid him in gold for the service of guiding her soul into the next world, but he was not in his homeland, and the government prohibited any sorcery. Only in America did he consider for the first time that this might not actually work. He was unsure whether this was because he was in a different land or a different time.

He observed the mourning period anyway and then went to see his Aunt Jean and Uncle Henry. Traditionally, that time could have lasted up to three years. Instead he held a month-long vigil. There were some blessings in modernity. The permits for the restaurant were ready and the remodeling about to begin, Uncle Henry had told him by phone. Saihung had seen the attractive storefront out on Clement Street. He had invested all his money, but it was for the best. He would have a secure future.

Uncle Henry and Aunt Jean's house was about an hour's walk from Chinatown. It was a two-story Italianate in the Marina district. He appreciated the sun and the fresh air that came to the front of the building. It was certainly better than Chinatown. He went up the stairs of the white stucco building and rang their bell. No response. He rang again. Saihung shrugged. He'd leave a note and call some other time.

As he turned, the landlady poked her head out the other door. She was a large Chinese woman who had plucked her natural eyebrows out in favor of higher, painted ones.

"You're making a great deal of noise," she said fearlessly.

"My apologies, I just came to see the Chans."

"Too late. They've moved." She began to close the door.

"Moved?" Saihung reached out to stop her. His heart began to beat faster.

"Yes. Two days ago. And don't try to rent their place either. I already have other prospects." She glared at him until he took his hand from the knob.

"But where did they move to? Did they leave an address?"

"No. What do I care?" She slammed the door.

Saihung stumbled dumbly down the stairs. He felt like an idiot, and reproached himself repeatedly. For all his time abroad, he had kept to himself, been very careful. He walked home from his aunt and uncle's house mournfully. He had been swindled out of his life's savings. There would be little hope of independence now.

He picked up his mail, climbed the long rickety stairs to his one room, and sat glumly on the creaking bed. He truly had nothing—only the money in his pocket. It would be two weeks to his next pay period and working as a waiter would bring little money in.

Saihung had been in the country nearly twenty years. Twenty years in which he did not fit in, twenty years in which he had felt alienated from his master, his past, the country that surrounded him. Twenty years in which he had seen people dear to him die just working their whole lives away. Twenty years struggling to establish himself only to have it swept away by greedy relatives.

It was twilight. An orange light came over the crest of the hill and the bells of the nearby cathedral began to ring. He drew the roller blind and looked helplessly around the room. He felt trapped in the cubicle. The brown and green wallpaper, yellowed by a film of nicotine from previous tenants, made the room seem smaller. The light was low—a brighter bulb would blow the fuses—and the sepia shadows seemed to wash in toward his feet. He kept the pale green portal of the door closed. It kept out the noise and the rats.

He picked forlornly through his mail, and brightened a bit upon seeing his master's calligraphy. He had written to his teacher, hoping for some wisdom, some guidance from the one he hoped would save him. Reverently, he turned on the gooseneck lamp on his battered desk and opened the envelope. He unfolded the white paper only to find one word brushed in powerful strokes.

"Persevere."

Saihung tore the letter up in anger.

He sat on the edge of the bed and tried to meditate. Nothing happened. All that came to him was a burning desire for revenge. There was no dodging this blow. He would suffer for a long time.

Saihung never found his swindlers, though he tried. Over the next few years, he patiently stalked them and traveled through much of the western United States. But they always stayed a step ahead of him, and eventually left the country. A sense of futility overtook Saihung, though his hatred soon faded into a simple sense of desperation. He truly had nothing. He could afford to eat only some canned food roughly overturned on a bowl of rice.

In spite of the despair that gripped him during that time, he was intrigued to find that his meditations grew more deep in the next year. He had nothing. He couldn't go out, he couldn't find any happiness. He craved a serenity free from any conscious thought. He had to make a living, fight enemies, face his problems. He had discovered his drives and ambitions, his own implicit qualities, saw the storehouse of attributes that he had accumulated. If only he could empty his mind completely of those things, then he could undoubtedly enjoy great peace. In earlier years, both on Huashan and in India, he had enjoyed such serenity. He wanted to find that tranquility again.

Whenever he was devoid of thoughts and appetites during meditation, he felt a great bliss. He began to meditate more. Every moment when he was not doing so was a moment of torture. Spiritual practice was addicting. It was a lie that holy men were all gentle and kind. Those he had known were among the most moody and angry men he had met. From hermits in China to sages in the Himalayas, they resented being torn away from their heavenly states. He never thought that he too would come to a point where everyday pain would increase his own need for meditation.

He wanted to be empty. That meant that the energy he cultivated, such as what he experienced while practicing Tai Chi, might then be used to empower introspection. For the Taoists, even looking within required an extraordinary amount of energy. No normal person could have the stamina to make the long inquiry. And more to the point, the mind had a variety of dimensions that the normal person did not even suspect.

Everyone talked about the self, from the most egotistical lout to the highest holy man. But his aim was to subdue the self, that part of him that was aware of his pain. His master told him in letters that the self did not exist in the first place. Why, then, should Saihung be so troubled? The difficulty, after all, was only imagined. There was no actual self to suffer. But how could he be nonexistent and aware of his apparent unreality? His master had only asked the simple question, "Are there two of you?" Saihung was an indivisible whole. His belief in a self was in itself a delusion. Once he understood that, his ignorance would fade away.

Return to the source. That was all that the Taoists seemed to repeat over and over. What was that source? It was supposedly a state of complete void. That was what he concentrated on day after day. Being a waiter was secondary. Being anything outside his room was nothing compared to what he was experiencing inside his mind. That room in Chinatown became his meditation cell, the place where he began to resolve all the various aspects of his life by first realizing that they were part of a whole that had never truly existed objectively.

He went on for months. In the profundity of these states of consciousness, he realized that his identity was fading. He had done it all. He had lived through the Sino-Japanese War and the revolution. He had been a Taoist, a politician, a martial artist, a waiter. Now he realized that those had been mere identities. Instead of defining him, they had discharged some aspect of his personality. Only a tiny bit—a thread—remained to pull his soul back into his body.

Since his youth, Saihung had learned that one of the highest accomplishments was to leave one's body. If the practitioner had substantially liberated himself from the attachments of life, and if he knew the correct procedure, he could project his spirit away from his body forever. Saihung wanted to do that. He felt close to that point. It would just take a little bit of effort and he could launch himself away from his misery and unhappiness. If he was successful, his physical body would apparently die, but the soul would be radiant, conscious, immortal. But there was a danger. After all, the universe and all the dimensions were infinitely vast, eternally complex. As wonderful an achievement as it was to liberate the soul from the body, there were many realities and many places of illusion; the fragile soul could be easily lost.

He needed his master. Even if he reached the stage of skill and eligibility, his master had to be on "the other side" to guide his soul to the correct gate. Otherwise, there would be enslavement by other beings or imprisonment in limbo. He poured out his troubles in a letter to his master, telling of his successes, begging his teacher to grant him the final act of grace. Expectantly, he entered each session of meditation, waiting for the last glorious moment when he would be shown the true portal.

For once, the Grand Master replied quickly. "I forbid you to leave. You have not determined your destiny, let alone fulfilled it. You have too many sorrows and regrets. Any one of those, unless resolved in actual life, can pull you back to earth. Resolve the turmoil in your heart." To add to the insult, he criticized Saihung's spelling and calligraphy.

Saihung promptly wrote back. "There is nothing in this world for me. I can see the gate and the world beyond it. I will go through whether you bless me or not."

The written reply was short and harsh. "No," the letter stated simply. "I will stop you."

Saihung furiously ripped the last letter up. He cursed his master as the cruelest old man who ever lived. It was easy for him, thought Saihung resentfully. The Grand

Master could undoubtedly visit any part of the universe he pleased. Time, space, and consciousness were no barriers for him. He probably cavorted with the gods themselves. But when it came to using his power to lift his youngest disciple from the wretchedness of the world, he was stingy and uncompassionate.

To hell with him! Saihung decided he would leave the world anyway. He doubted that the Grand Master could stop him. The Grand Master had threatened to place a barrier over Saihung's soul, barring his exit from the world. That would have been a tremendous act of power and Saihung judged that his master might not be capable of it. He decided that it was just a psychological threat. He would redouble his efforts and discover in space whether there could be such a wall.

Within forty more days, he came closer and closer to leaving his body. He quit his job so that he could meditate four days a week. He ate very little, only enough to keep his body going. He would soon enter a stage where he would not eat at all or go out. He floated in a state of bliss, already halfway in the next world.

Nine days more and the process would be complete. He meditated on. The night of the forty-eighth day, his spirit rose up from his body. Radiant. Shining. Pure. Who could doubt that there was a self?

He was a bright star floating upward. He was pure energy, pure being. In the dark hotel room, he seemed to float as if in an aqueous medium. He looked down at his body, sitting there very still. He felt curious, wondering whether this was actually himself. Here he was, looking at his own body in the only way to do so beside using a reflection. What was sitting there couldn't be him, if what was looking was the consciousness floating above. The body was not the self, he concluded.

The dazzling light within him continued. The walls seemed to be nothing. They were only composed of matter. He was now pure consciousness, and nothing on the material plane could oppose him. They dissolved.

He was out in darkness. Saihung felt an acceleration, and he burst into a maelstrom of colors. Colors more vivid than dyed silk, more brilliant than the refractions from a thousand shattered prism spectrums. He flew through this vortex effortlessly, powerfully. After some distance, he came to an opening into a boundless space. There, across this ocean of molten rainbows, he saw the gate to liberation.

He floated in utter tranquility, and it seemed that his entire soul trembled in the delight of experiencing a splendor that was holy, welcome, and peaceful. He was light, and he absorbed light, became brighter as he went closer. He felt a profound sobriety. It was an aloofness from all that was human, all that was associated with the misery of his emotions and the tyranny of his subjectivity. He was free simply to perceive the gentle thrill of being in a stream of infinity. He was with the Tao.

Saihung contemplated this opening in space. He wanted very much to go through it and leave the human world behind. There was a wide world on the other side, a paradise. It was not like the human world at all. It was no city, no place, not material. It was not even governed by the physics that people experienced. Nevertheless, Saihung felt himself overwhelmingly attracted to it. He let himself go with no regrets, no hesitation. Now! He would leave this human folly for all eternity!

He willed himself forward, farther than he had ever projected himself. Recklessly, he plunged further. He strained his concentration, kept it at an absolute peak. The silver cord that attached him to his body, that was literally his very lifeline back to earth, began to stretch very thin and fade in its luster. Saihung was taking a very dangerous gamble, but his eagerness was uncontainable. He flew toward the portal.

Suddenly, the jarring sound of an electric guitar chord cut his trajectory. He felt pain. The place where the silver cord was attached to his abdomen wrenched at him and he turned in space. Again came the noise, and he was jerked back into his body so suddenly that he nearly cried out with the agony. He opened his eyes. He was back in the room. His neighbor next door had chosen that moment to turn his radio up loudly. Rock music blasted through the walls so acutely that the walls shook.

He lost all control. Saihung dashed from his room, his eyes glaring demonically. He splintered his neighbor's door. With a mighty grip, he pulled the startled man to his feet. He prepared to smash his fist to the neighbor's face, even as the man wet his pants in terror.

"He's killing me!" The neighbor's eyes teared up with fear, and Saihung could feel his stiff neck trembling under his grip. Saihung squeezed a bit more to quiet him. The wire-framed glasses the skinny, balding man was wearing fell to the floor.

Other men came at their neighbor's call, and they desperately tried to separate Saihung from the frightened man. It took six men to drag him into the hallway. He let them do it, for he had slowly begun to realize the absurdity of his actions.

The manager, an overweight ex-Marine, told him to move. He would not have maniacs busting down doors. Saihung didn't care. That day was the forty-ninth. He would be gone by the evening.

He sat back down in his room. The floor was fearfully quiet. There was no doubt: He had to leave the world. But when he tried to enter into the special state of serenity, he found that it was impossible. In losing his temper, he had lost the delicate detachment that made him eligible to leave his body. The feelings of meditation, all that he had experienced, was gone.

Perseverance

The only thing that had stopped Saihung from leaving his body forever had been the radio. He found another flophouse hotel in which to live, and went to work at a liquor store. He wanted to try again. But this time he would plan his physical environment much more carefully. Saihung resolved that he would find the proper atmosphere, not some urban place, but consecrated ground where no interruptions would occur.

The ideal place would be a temple or hermitage. Saihung had a friend, the abbot of a Zen temple in Japan. He wrote to the priest, honestly disclosing his intention to leave his body. That request was proper, but not all holy people believed in voluntarily forsaking the world. It was with great relief that he received the reply. The abbot consented.

Again, the possibility of leaving the world became practical. Saihung went for a walk to think things over. He enjoyed the clear sunshine and found himself climbing the slopes of Telegraph Hill. He walked up the Filbert Street steps. It was distant from Huashan, he thought, but here he was, again climbing a mountain.

He walked the path that spiraled around Coit Tower. He saw a few tourists, and couples in love. Children were playing in the shrubbery. He had a commanding view of the city, the Golden Gate, the shimmering bay. The moon had already risen, a pale white disc against the powder blue sky. A pair of sparrows flew by him. They landed on the branch of a green bush with red berries, and scrutinized him, turning their heads in short gestures. Life was not any less delightful, he had to admit, but it no longer had much appeal for him.

Saihung took the letter from his pocket and read it again. Yes, he decided, here was his chance to attempt another departure. Once he was in the serenity of a temple, he could achieve the proper consciousness. There would be no desperate circumstances, no noisy neighbors. He planned to save enough money to make the journey, make a donation to the temple, and leave enough behind to provide for the Grand Master and the two acolytes. He would leave the world with no doubts.

He considered that he had not completed his assigned quest. He had come no closer to saying the answer that his master expected. He still had no idea of what it might be—perhaps it wasn't anything verbal. The most eloquent answer would have to be his life. He had struggled and fallen from the path repeatedly. He had traveled around the world, known wealth and poverty, wisdom and ignorance. He had maintained his body in meticulous health, and it had served him in martial arts duels, Golden Gloves bouts, and brawls in the street. He had shaped it into a cocoon, in preparation for his ascension.

His Taoist name was the Butterfly Taoist. He had always been a little ambivalent about it. It certainly wasn't a masculine name. But it perfectly expressed this climax to his life. Maybe the Grand Master had even foreseen it when naming him. Perhaps the Butterfly had prepared himself for a second birth. That was surely as noble a destiny as any.

He decided that this would be what he would tell his master. Hopefully, it would placate the Grand Master enough for him to guide Saihung's soul away. After all, he wouldn't even be the first. Out of thirteen classmates, the Grand Master had already ushered eight from their bodies. It was unfair of him to deny Saihung alone. If Saihung could not join his master in China, then he would await him in the next world.

He sighed. Renunciation and liberation were only for the world-weary, he reflected. When he was younger, the world seemed so thrilling. The political shifting and acceleration of technological societies had coincided with his disillusionment. There was really no reason to curse progress. It was wonderful for those who could benefit from it and find delight in it. There was nothing wrong with it. But it had hastened his own alienation. For centuries, literature had alluded to the red dust of the world. The red dust had choked him long enough. He was ready to shake it off. The Butterfly was ready to fly.

A voice interrupted his thoughts.

"Hey! Hi! How ya doin'?"

Saihung looked up, startled. He quickly put away the letter.

"Remember me? My name's Steve. I come to the liquor store."

"Right. I remember you," replied Saihung. He looked at the slender, handsome Eurasian. Steve had long, shoulder-length hair, black-rimmed aviator glasses. He wore Ben Davis pants and basketball shoes. His T-shirt had a peace symbol on it. Saihung knew him to be in his twenties, or at least he had a fake I.D. that said so.

Steve sat down casually on the bench without asking. Saihung hid his annoyance.

"What's your name, man?" asked Steve.

"Kwan."

"Hey, far out. Like the god of war, right?" Steve had an exaggeratedly mellow tone to his voice. It irritated Saihung.

"Sort of," replied Saihung disinterestedly.

"Yeah. Hey, Kwan, want a toke?" Steve took a carefully rolled joint from a matchbox. Saihung refused.

"It's really good. Heavy with resin. It ain't no seeds and stems. You could really get off on it. Maybe see things, huh?"

Saihung only smiled weakly. He hadn't heard this type of talk in movies, and his curiosity about Steve's odd language was the only thing that kept him from being rude.

"Yeah, I like to come up here a lot," continued Steve. "Get my head together. It's like, you know, going to higher ground." Steve leaned back on the bench and looked wistfully to the horizon.

"Yes . . . Yeah," Saihung replied, trying to imitate the kid's talk.

"So you wanna get high?"

"No," said Saihung with a weak excuse. "I'm allergic."

"Oh. OK. Hey, I'll just take a walk and come back. Don't go away, OK, Kwan?"

"OK," said Saihung without hesitation. He did not think to turn down such an innocent request. He had a soft spot for kids.

He watched Steve walk to the base of a eucalyptus tree to light up. What a waste, thought Saihung. Instinctively, he scanned Steve's body. It was a martial habit to check every person's weaknesses. Steve was clearly no threat, but he seemed healthy. If only he knew how to take care of himself, he could realize his potential, thought Saihung. He wondered about Steve's Eurasian background, and was reminded of men in the Chinese aristocracy who had arranged to have European mistresses. They wanted children with the minds and thinking of Chinese, but the strength and beauty of Europeans. Breeding super children was the way they hoped to perpetuate their class. Saihung had known some of the children while growing up, and had watched with pity as they had been rejected by both cultures. Steve was clearly not the result of such a bizarre sociobiological experiment, but Saihung sensed that he suffered the same problems of dual rejection.

"Hey thanks for waiting, man," said Steve, returning red-eyed.

Saihung should have gotten up and left, prepared for his trip to Japan. He didn't know why he stayed.

"Feel better?" No use sermonizing, thought Saihung.

"Yeah. Great!" There was a pause as he savored his euphoria.

"Did you see that movie down at the Great Star Theater?" asked Steve. "Man, those movies are fantastic!"

He was talking about martial arts movies. Saihung laughed. The movies were a pale image of the great martial world he had known.

"I saw *Five Fingers of Death* ten times!" continued Steve enthusiastically. "I was trying to learn some moves. Like this. Check this out!"

Steven ran through some strikes and kicks with great seriousness. Saihung found them hilarious, but maintained a polite demeanor.

"How 'bout that, Kwan? Does it look like the real thing?"

"Uh . . . I don't know." Saihung smiled, and tried to be diplomatic. "Maybe the stance isn't very good."

"I couldn't see that part. It was a close-up."

Saihung laughed out loud. He didn't know what made him stand up. Perhaps it was Steve's innocence. He checked to see if anyone was looking, and when he saw that no one was, he launched into a short performance of Lost Track Boxing.

"Wow! Wow! Hey Kwan, that's spectacular! Teach me! Teach me!"

"I don't know anything," said Saihung, regretting his lapse.

"You do! You do!"

Saihung vacillated. He shouldn't have shown anything. But the boy was so earnest. "Why don't you join a school?" asked Saihung.

Steve grew quiet. "Oh, I don't know . . . no money . . . wouldn't fit in . . . you know."

Saihung felt sympathetic. He paused for a moment. There was absolutely no rational reason why he should make any offer, but without consideration, he said, "I've got a couple hours off tomorrow. Want to meet here?"

He was gratified by a beautiful and appreciative smile. "I guess I should kneel down, huh?"

"Don't do anything like that," said Saihung hastily. "Let's just say we're working out together. We're trading knowledge. Maybe there's something that you can show me."

"I don't know anything," said Steve dubiously. "This doesn't mean you're not going to show me anything, does it?"

"Of course not," explained Saihung patiently. "But let me tell you something about myself. That way, no one's disappointed. Fair enough?"

Steve nodded.

"I'm a wanderer," said Saihung. "I can show you things you never even dreamed about, but that doesn't mean that I'm a mystical being. I'm only an ordinary man. Remember that, all right?"

"That's good enough for me," Steve said enthusiastically.

"OK. I'll see you tomorrow." He began walking down the hill.

"Thanks, man," shouted Steve behind him.

Saihung had not had any martial arts students since he had left China. He liked having students in a way, for he had a strong paternal streak, but he had not considered teaching for nearly three decades. He had established that he had only wanted liberation. That required having no commitments. Having students was a big responsibility.

Taoists traditionally met students by chance. The meeting of an anonymous traveling Taoist was so common in classical literature that it was a cliché. Even Saihung's own study had come from such a seemingly random meeting. The stories always spoke of the great difference that Taoist wisdom made on the recipient. Nowhere, Saihung thought, did they ever focus on the other side. He could recall no story where they talked about how the Taoist felt.

Saihung knew that the Taoist was not supposed to feel anything. He was supposedly above such follies. The Taoist, upon meeting someone in need, was to share his knowledge out of unselfish compassion. After the circumstances in question were settled, they disappeared. A Taoist was nonattached. Unconcerned about worldly things and human emotions, the true wandering Taoist never sought to have a following or set himself upon some throne of permanency. Presumably, he walked away and forgot the whole incident. It was, after all, not even real to him.

He had now come together by chance with a person in need. It was right to help another, he told himself. He could always leave. He wrote his master for advice after he began teaching Steve. Should he leave his body or stay and teach? Steve would never be a Taoist, and Saihung was undecided about what to do.

The Grand Master's reply was considerate and gentle. He felt that Saihung would make a good teacher. Saihung was quizzical about this. He felt that he had no patience.

"It is not your time to leave your body," the Grand Master reminded him. "Death is preordained and we cannot alter that. You are under no compulsion to teach. But it is noble to help another.

"You have the personality for it. You won't frighten your students. Teaching is not your ultimate destiny, but if you stop and think, you'll realize that you haven't completed everything yet. Complete your life before you try to leave it behind."

Saihung pondered his master's words. He had grown tired of the grotesque human carnival. He had exhausted the depths and breadths of life. Leaving had been his primary concern and the only way to leave life was death. But how to die was the question. Everyone had a different way, he thought. Some died in their sleep, some died in violent accidents. Some died for a cause, others with whimpering and tears. Most did not even know how death finally overtook them, and were ground beneath the wheel of transmigration again. He had wanted to make his final worldly act the conscious and beautiful act of leaving his body.

Yet, that was still death. He knew if he had broken the Grand Master's prohibition and had rushed into the void that he would not likely have reached the gate. He admitted to himself that he would have been committing suicide. That would have been a waste, and it would have condemned him to rebirth—if his soul had been collected.

Saihung sat down to meditate. He would not try to leave, would not try to accomplish anything, he told himself. He touched his fingers together, his thumbs, palms, and overlapped fingers formed a circle. He let his eyes almost close, and focused them on the floor a few feet in front of him. Gradually, he put his thought on his breathing, letting his breath settle into a slow and deep cycle. The more his inhalations and exhalations lengthened, the more his mind became calm.

Years ago, his master had asked him if he existed. He considered this question again. The body that had been his haven and his vehicle of martial pride was something he had been eager to leave behind. He had seen the spirit rise from the body. Thus he concluded that the body was not his true self. It would fall as soon as he flew. Decay would begin immediately. It would separate into water, chemicals, particles. Surely then, the self might be the astral body that had risen into the room. But that spirit had consciousness and volition. He had been able to see his physical form and he had been able to travel. In essence, the self that emerged had a mind, or more precisely, was the mind.

Where was his mind, he asked himself. Where was the source of his consciousness?

He waited. No answer.

Where was the mind, he asked again.

No answer.

He felt a shimmer in him. The soul. The mind and the soul were one and the same. Not just the mind of the brain, but the greater mind that was a little blob of life force from the universal One.

Finally he knew that the brightness left after all other aspects of his life were stripped away was itself but a tiny distant reflection of the cosmic and almighty unity, a dew drop away from the shining ocean. Did he exist? No. Not once he understood that the concept of his individuality was a mistake. Not once he accepted that he was a part of all and all was a part of him. Separateness was only an illusion.

As he met Steve the next day, he realized what a pleasure it was to share, and he understood how long he had been without such a simple pleasure. It seemed to him that he had struggled in isolation since he had left China, and it had made him humorless and angry.

He watched Steve practicing the beginnings of the martial movements that Saihung had learned from Wang Ziping. On the green lawn overlooking the bay, with all of the office buildings and the waterfront below them, Steve slowly began to piece together the punches and variations in stance. Saihung thought of the long road ahead for Steve. It would take decades before the young man could do what Saihung did as a matter of reflex and instinct. But that was all right. Watching his student was like watching a baby learning to walk. There was still something delightful, joyous, an event that filled him with wonder.

Steve moved to the side in a lunge and whipped both arms like a windmill. His fists came into alignment, one in front, and one in back of him.

"Is it like this?" asked Steve.

Saihung silently went up to his pupil and raised the hands a little higher. He remembered how he himself would have been whipped with a split bamboo cane for such a simple question.

Steve moved into the next section of movements, moving in great sincerity, if not accuracy. He stopped.

"I don't remember this next part," he said apprehensively. It was a question that he seemed afraid to ask.

Saihung did not want to tell him that he himself had also been scared to ask the same questions of his teachers. He decided in that instant that he would not teach the way he had been taught.

"It's like this," said Saihung, as he leapt forward like an archer pulling a bow. He swiveled quickly and punched, twisted into a jumping kick, and came down into a combination of thrusts. Steve smiled happily.

"Do it with me," Saihung urged. Steve followed him as best as he could, and they did it over and over until the youth was breathless.

"I guess I'm a little out of shape." Steve bent over and put his hands on his knees.

"You have no stamina. Smoking and drinking destroy stamina." Saihung tried not to lecture. He still thought of himself as a student. He knew very well what treatment he resented, how reproaches could be confusing.

"Don't you work in a liquor store?" The boy pushed his glasses back onto his nose and turned to look at him.

"It's a job. I do it to survive. But I don't drink, smoke, or fool around with women."

"Never?" Steve looked at Saihung incredulously. "Man, isn't that a little grim?"

"No it isn't," said Saihung without hesitation. "In my time, there were many men like that. I had good examples. They inspired me to be this way. They taught me to walk this path, and I would never really consider leaving it. I have a master in China. He keeps me on the proper way. I control my diet, practice hygiene, exercise. That's it. Martial arts is only a hobby with me."

Steve straightened up. "Not a bad hobby. But what else do you do?"

"Meditation. That and philosophy are more important than fighting."

"I wish I could see you fight."

Saihung looked at Steve. "No you don't. You don't want to see me fight. There's nothing pretty about fighting. It's not a movie, it's not opera. And I don't want to ever catch you fighting either."

"But then why am I learning this?" Steve looked at him with a pout.

"As a means of discipline," replied Saihung. "If you learn martial arts, it will improve your health and give you the discipline to do anything in life. The demands to master all the facets of martial arts will shape your personality and give you the resources to face all that fate sends your way."

"How will it do that?"

"If you acquire discipline, then you will have the freedom to do anything and be anything you want in life. Then you can walk through a whole wonderful world that you'd never suspect existed. That's not the world of boxing, it's the world of experience. Life is the best teacher, and I am trying to equip you not to fight, but to learn from the true teacher."

"I'm not sure what you mean, but it sounds all right. Will you help me?"

"Sure, I will. But you have to put in the effort."

Steve nodded. "I will."

"OK. Back to practice."

They worked out together until the sky began to flame with the setting sun.

"That's it for today," said Saihung.

"Will you be here tomorrow?"

"Of course I will." Inwardly, Saihung knew that he was taking on another obligation.

"Can I bring a friend?"

"I don't know," said Saihung dubiously. This was a little too fast for him.

"Oh, please." Steve gave Saihung a pleading look. "He wants to learn too."

Saihung had many accomplishments, but disappointing young people was not among them. He tried to be strict. "We'll see."

"Great! See you tomorrow at the same time?"

"Yes, the same time."

Saihung watched the lanky boy trot contentedly down the hill. He laughed at himself for the talk that he had given Steve. Wasn't that what he himself needed to pull out of his desperate outlook? With a student, life did not seem so bleak or lonely. More importantly, it was a thrill to share the art that he cherished with someone who was falling in love with it for the first time. That freshness was a source of renewal for him.

Saihung sat down on a bench to watch the sun go down. He saw the orange orb slowly descend to the gray blue horizon, watched the deepening purple shadows of the streaked clouds. The sphere of fire was on the Pacific in a short time, but the combination of the two antagonistic elements seemed perfectly fine. He had a sense of harmony, and he felt his patience returning to him. He would continue to search for the answer that would satisfy his master, and in that process, find his own life's meaning as well. He stopped wanting to rush. There was time. And along the way, he would show this boy, and perhaps others, some of the beautiful secrets of life that he had spent a lifetime collecting. He would show them the way to a vast world.

Afterword

I stood on a busy Chinatown street, waiting for Mr. Kwan. He lived in a small, dark hotel. He could afford nothing else. I looked up at the pale pink stucco building and saw the opaque windows, wondering which room he was in and whether he could see me. I had come to help him run some errands before the small class that he taught. Though the time was prearranged, I did not ring or go to his room. He was late. Anticipating a long wait, I thought about my relationship with him.

I had seen his class almost accidentally while accompanying two friends. Not only did the beauty and vigor of the movements impress me, but I was also quite taken with the curriculum. Many of the arts that Mr. Kwan taught were only hinted about in books, or labeled "lost" or "legendary." Since my initial research into Chinese martial arts and Taoism, I had heard of boxing skills like Eight Trigrams Palm, or Snake Boxing; health exercises like Eight Pieces of Brocade, Muscle Change Classic, and the Five Animal Frolics; meditations such as the Eight Psychic Meridians Standing Meditation, and the Microcosmic Orbit. I had wanted to learn them for years.

I had read about the famous Song dynasty general Yueh Fei; now here was someone who knew his boxing style. I had read about the heroes of the classic *Water Margin*; now here was someone who knew how to use their strange weapons. I had heard of the famous Taoist strategist Zhu Geliang; now here was someone who had studied similar philosophies. Scholarly and military talents was the classical ideal in Imperial China. Mr. Kwan advocated that well, and he embodied a history's worth of ancient arts to support that. The chance of gaining a character of honor and dignity through martial arts, health through breathing and special gymnastics, and greater mental perception through meditation was very appealing to me.

Admittedly, my infatuation with martial arts was somewhat romantic, even unrealistic. I was addicted to Chinese novels about chivalry, honor, knights, and heroes. Many of these stories had supernatural elements—ghosts, goblins, demons, sorcerers—and Taoists. Usually, these men were considered to have great skill, magic arts, and an otherworldly perception that held this world as illusory. Taoism was present in much literature—from Chuang Tzu and Lao Tzu as opera characters, to the story of Han Chungli in the *Yellow Millet Dream*. A Taoist usually represented wisdom, nonconformity, and disinterested heroism. They often appeared in people's lives to intercede at just the right moment. With this cultural precedent, I was predisposed toward meeting a Taoist.

When I began to study with Mr. Kwan, all these elements fell into proper place. With some background and need within me, I naturally worked harder to progress in the system. I found to my great delight that it was not only possible to learn the many things I wanted, but that they could be combined in a systematic way as well. Mr. Kwan began from the simple premise that the body had first to be made into a fit vehicle for the mind and spirit. I learned calisthenics, stretches, different kinds of boxing. The breath needed to be trained, so I learned a great variety of breathing movements that attempted to direct the flow of physical energy in the body (*qigong*). He did not teach philosophy by discourse; I simply accompanied him and learned from his reaction to actual life experiences. Meditation would not be taught until he believed me to be thoroughly prepared (it would be years).

I had frankly been disappointed by nearly every teacher and religious figure I had encountered. Mr. Kwan could well have been a charlatan in search of an easy ride. But living in a cheap rooming house was no easy ride for anyone. He would never get rich teaching martial arts, and there was no sane reason for someone to put up with the difficulties of teaching and maintaining the lifestyle he advocated when there were considerably more comfortable options.

More important were Mr. Kwan's abilities. Though he maintained a very low profile, it was always a revelation whenever some hidden facet of his personality would show for a moment. His metaphysical discussions were not only enlightening, but virtually invulnerable to argument. His depth of knowledge of Chinese culture was amazing. He knew things even my grandmother didn't know, and in some ways was even more traditional and conservative than she. Whenever I thought back on the times he had thrown or struck me during a demonstration, my doubts faded. Skill was always apparent. One could not fake talent.

Hearing of his travels in the United States, I knew he had had to make compromises, and inevitable mistakes. Perhaps some would have said that he was not even "spiritual." Someone who fought in the streets, worked as a cook and a waiter, who scraped for his existence like many other immigrants, may not have fit their preconceptions of a holy aspirant. But good fortune and a life devoid of doubt and conflict seldom happen to a person who faces life's deepest questions. What is "spiritual" is an arbitrary and often impossibly utopian notion defined by people—no god ever wrote a scripture. Spirituality that is never tested by bitterness, that never has to face the dilemmas of contradictory experiences, can never be strong, true, or honest.

Such integrity was undoubtedly all that Mr. Kwan cared about. For him, spirituality was not a fantasy. He made it clear that he did not consider himself to be special. Mr. Kwan said that his only secrets were that he kept to the way of his master's lineage, kept himself healthy, sought the reasons for his life, and helped those whom he met without seeking to bind them to himself. His Taoism was a hardheaded, practical, hardworking, and disciplined system. He advocated celibacy, abstention from liquor, drugs, certain meats, bad thinking, and overinvolvement with worldly things. All there was for him was daily practice, discipline, dignity, understanding.

Following him required considerable sacrifice on the part of the prospective student. I was not surprised by the number of students who left him—dozens more than stayed. They refused to make the sacrifices and put aside enjoyments, relationships, or careers goals. Mr. Kwan told me that since not everyone is ready to learn or stay, he can do nothing but let them go. I once thought this sad, but after many years I had to conclude that he was right.

I made my own sacrifices, though they were always gradual and voluntary. One of them involved drinking, which I loved. When I began to learn qigong, Mr. Kwan warned me to stop. Once purified, the body would reject all that was bad for it. I scoffed inwardly at this advice. Who could be sure if all this huffing and puffing and holding of the breath would have an effect? I would wait and see. The desire to have my cake and eat it too was always an unfortunate tendency.

Before long, I found that I could not hold my liquor as before, and worse, the pleasure faded. It might just be psychological, I reasoned. Stubbornly, I refused to change until a crisis brought on a decision.

Mr. Kwan was far away on a long journey. I had just moved into a house and was due to have a big party the next day. I became violently sick, enough that I woke up in agony. The party could be canceled, of course, but I did not want such an embarrassment. Nevertheless, I could not see the possibility of recovering in time as I knelt at the toilet, waiting in high fever to throw up. I hated nausea. I hated vomiting. As I lapsed into dry heaves, I blamed Mr. Kwan.

"I know you're doing this to me," I said superstitiously. "Or at least someone up there is. All right. I'll make a deal. Let me get well in time for my party and I'll quit drinking."

The next day, to my great chagrin, I was well. I decided to keep my promise—it was as good an excuse as any—and all my friends were shocked at my sobriety that night.

Once I made this sacrifice, it became a little easier to make others. Gradually I tried to make my life more in keeping with the way I was learning. I made many mistakes, of course, but persevered. Mr. Kwan always emphasized discipline. From my sacrifices, I realized that discipline was equivalent to freedom. Pure self-denial does not have any intrinsic value, but discipline and self-control allow one to set a goal and do the necessary things to attain it. I valued my relationship with Mr. Kwan, and that was part of the reason that I did not mind waiting ridiculously on a Chinatown street.

Mr. Kwan finally came down the stairs, and I put aside my reflections. He was dressed in warm-up clothes and running shoes. His face was wide, rectangular, red. The feature that always struck me were his large glistening eyes. As he crossed the street, my heart sank. I could see that he was in a bad mood.

"Sifu," I greeted him respectfully.

"These people don't know who they're pushing around," he began without preliminaries.

What had happened? Had he gotten into some trouble? Had he thrashed someone in the streets? It wasn't considered polite to ask.

"Are you having some difficulty?" I asked carefully.

Mr. Kwan caught himself. "Oh, never mind," he said. "I must be the only practitioner who has to scrounge for his own existence. But I have to talk to you."

I was surprised. He was seldom so direct.

"They've taken everything away from me in this country. I've been discriminated against. I've lost so much. But I want to give you something that can't be taken away."

"What is it, Sifu?" I hoped it wasn't too valuable. I had a tendency to lose things. Perhaps I could get a safe-deposit box.

"A spiritual legacy. You have a father. Someday he will give you an inheritance. That will be your material legacy. But a master is like a spiritual father. His heritage is spiritual. This is transmitted from the master to the student. It is inside. They cannot take it away, yet it is a great gift."

I could not believe what he was offering to me. "I will try my best, Sifu," I said immediately.

"Good. Let's go shopping."

We got into my car. He had asked me to make a commitment. I had made it. I should go into this new stage in my life with no doubts, I told myself.

"Sifu?" I asked before I started the car.

"Yes?"

"There's just one question I would like to ask."

"OK."

"Did you do anything to make me stop drinking?"

He began laughing hysterically. The normally stoic Mr. Kwan turned scarlet from giggling.

"I would not use sorcery on you, even if I knew it," said Mr. Kwan when he had collected himself. "You are a young man, already half-formed. You know how to make decisions in your life. It would be wrong for me to bewitch you because you would never understand the reason you were doing something. I can only make suggestions and hope you'll listen. If you were a child, it would be different. If the child does something wrong, the elder punishes the child. If I treated you the same way, you would only resent it.

"I need you to cooperate. You must make the effort. I'm not pouring anything into you. You are creating yourself. I am like a sculptor. He takes a little here, adds a little there, but he cannot change the inherent nature of his material."

I became the sculpture who participated in its own sculpting and it was the beginning of a great deepening in my learning. It was said that one could not learn without the grace of the master. It was true. Though I might find a procedure published in a book, it didn't seem to work until it was taught to me—and invariably details were left out of the writing. I suppose this was what is called "direct transmission." It wasn't anything mystical or supernatural. It was the security and power of a lineage, the outside-the-self vitality of being taught. It was for that very reason that the self-taught are inherently boring.

Some of the best lessons happened spontaneously. I remember, for example, his lesson to me about *yin* and *yang*. We were sitting in my parked car and began discussing the fundamental duality of the universe. Though it was hardly the traditional poetic spot by a mountain waterfall, we fell into discussion. "*Yin* is like all these moving cars and rushing people," Mr. Kwan said. "*Yang* is like that phone pole."

I was puzzled. I quickly reviewed what I had learned about *yin* and *yang*—something I only knew from reading. I wondered what direct experience could lead him to say such a bizarre sentence.

All I knew about *yin* and *yang* was that *yang* was all things positive: light, hardness, fire, movement. *Yin* was negative: darkness, softness, water, stillness. There was certainly nothing in the classical references that would have led me to cars and phone poles. I really didn't understand him, and asked for further explanation.

"*Yin* represents ambition, drive, movement," Mr. Kwan told me. "It is the female, the ultimate fertility. *Yang*, by itself, is so strong, but in its pure form it has no drive, no motivation. Thus it is static: without *yin* it cannot move. Without *yang*, *yin* will have neither direction nor form."

"*Yin* is movement, *yang* is stillness?" I asked. "You are saying the opposite of what is written in the books."

"That's why book learning is inadequate," he said dryly. "I only learned that lesson from two Taoists with whom I traveled. They told me that the lessons of life were far superior to the words of men. According to my masters, life is the only true classroom and experience is the only reliable textbook."

Real-life situations were what Mr. Kwan liked best. The Tao was everywhere. Its understanding was to be imparted at any time. Theory was important, but a book could not shock one out of one's misconceptions like a teacher could. This could happen anytime and anywhere—even after a movie.

"Casanova is the perfect Taoist," Mr. Kwan declared after we had seen the film *La Nuit de Varennes*. I was mystified again. How could a man like Mr. Kwan, raised in a monastery, advocating a lifestyle of meditation, discipline, and celibacy, call Casanova a perfect Taoist?

"Are you sure?" I asked him. "He seems to be a self-indulgent seducer."

"But he had insight," replied Mr. Kwan firmly. "He perceived his own nature and did not hesitate to fulfill his destiny. He was a free-thinker and a man of high cultivation. That's why I call him a perfect Taoist."

Mr. Kwan's pragmatism sometimes meant that his lessons were on a martial level. At one point, there had been an outbreak of muggings on buses. Mr. Kwan came to class one night with great concern. He had us set up chairs to imitate a bus and we went through hours of drilling to cover every aspect of attack on public transportation. He even taught the women separate techniques, going as far as borrowing a purse to show its use as a weapon. Eventually, we moved to strategies that had evolved from his experiences in New York. Significantly, that was the first time we had even heard of his stay in New York. We still have a technique that is nicknamed "The New York Subway," instead of its original and more poetic name "The Crimson Child Worships Buddha."

Just because Mr. Kwan decided to teach me (as he has others) doesn't mean the way has been any easier. I got no breaks. Everything I accomplished, I had to do on my own. He opened the door, I had to walk through. He set the tests, I had to pass them. Master and student walk the path side by side. While they walk, neither is to deter the other. The master tries to help, as long as it does not interfere with his own journey. The student tries to reciprocate. Mr. Kwan tried his best to teach me, yet I was always under the impression that if I left the path it would have been because I faltered, or my destiny ran out, not because the way was not open to me.

I remained ordinary; nothing mystical ever happened to me. Compared to some classmates and other students Mr. Kwan has had, I fell below average. Some procedures I frankly failed at, even after years of constant attempt. I still dropped my breakfast on the floor, took the garbage out myself. Even pride was denied to me. Mr. Kwan was always around to reinforce humility, and I lived with a cat who gave his literary criticism by sitting on my latest manuscript.

Yet after all this time in study, I have reached a few opinions. Perhaps one would think that I hold to fancy quotes from abstruse scriptures, or that I find some special meaning in esoteric practices. My conclusion is, however, considerably more mundane. Quite simply, I can summarize all my years of study by this one phrase: Have a goal in life.

It may sound stupidly simple, but that's it. The Tao is a way. What have you to walk but your life's path? There is no other way to gauge your progress along this path than to keep your goal in mind. This goal must be found within. It is not something shallow like "I want to be an artist," but it's something unique to you. Each person has some special destiny to fulfill, and the Taoists believe that it is imperative to find that fulfillment before death comes.

Even Mr. Kwan's own struggle and quest continues. His master, still alive in China today, refuses to let him come home: He still has not gotten the answer. Whatever this task is, it is something far beyond mundane realization, enlightenment, or the completion of errands. I am not inviting the reader to guess what Mr. Kwan's destiny is. Rather, I invite you to think of your own. We must all walk our life's way, solve our own personal riddle. If someone like Mr. Kwan can persevere with undiminished determination, then surely the rest of us can put aside the petty and banal details of every day to pursue our highest goal.

All the special methods of Taoism are relevant only because they help to clarify and achieve that goal. A Taoist must endure suffering and misfortune like anyone else. The only difference is that Taoists believe in having many skills and resources to traverse this uncertain life. There is no such thing as predestination, though the Taoists use the term poetically. No one knows beforehand what circumstances will befall oneself. But whatever they may be, the Taoists hope to have whatever means necessary to maintain their purpose. That is the meaning of the Taoist maxim, "Know magic, shun magic."

This focus on a goal should not be the adaptation of an identity. Quite the opposite. Taoism teaches the gradual fulfillment of one's life task along with simultaneous detachment from worldly priorities. At this point, meditation becomes supreme. Each person has a human identity. That self has to be understood. Once its mystery is illuminated, one can forsake identification with the world and the self. This identification is our bondage. If we free ourselves from such bondage, the liberated soul returns to its source. That source is Nothingness.

The self is intricate and complex. Only meditation can lead through the many, many layers of the self. These layers should not be conceived in a two- nor even a three-dimensional way. Rather, each strata of the self is infinite in its potential parameters. If one begins to explore even the most esoteric dimensions of the mind—psychic powers, for example—there is a danger that one will come to identify with such powers and forget the ultimate importance of simplicity and nonattachment to an identity. One may even continue on to eternity in the thrilling vistas of the mind (perhaps even becoming a god), but one will fail to find any unity with the cosmos because one is completely involved in self-love. This is what it means to fall into delusion. Only by entering stillness and looking within can one adequately bring forth the hidden mysteries and powers of the mind, examine them, and then discard them. Only through meditation can we avoid entrapment in the labyrinth of the mind. Only in meditation can we dissolve the personality.

I cannot describe any further. I still lack experience. But you can see that this practice is unlike the stereotyped concepts about Taoism. Since the practice aims at letting go of one's identity, it would be absurd to rush out to become a Taoist. The Taoist way is to simplify and avoid identity. Forget the robes and yin-yang symbols and all the strange mumblings. Forget being part of some mighty society. Taoism offers only progressive simplification past the point of zero.

It surprises me that I've written this much. I consider my time with Mr. Kwan very special and private. Perhaps I am not as compassionate as he is; I don't think I would reveal my study as he has allowed his to be revealed. I've written the *Chronicles of Tao* to support him and honor his tradition, to show that the antiquity he so treasures is being perpetuated. The fact that his system is still alive and vital is not the impossible replication of old Taoism. Rather, it is the nurturing of a seed from that great tree. Should it sprout and grow to maturity, it will be the spiritual legacy that he promised me.

Mr. Kwan has retired now, weary of his trials in the world, unwilling to advocate his calling publicly. He has withdrawn into seclusion for his final stage. But I feel fortunate. I have found a way of life that guides and sustains me. I value this heritage, and finally understand why the masters would rather it died than permit its adulteration. I will walk my path as long as I am permitted, in reverence for the beauty being constantly born, and the way of the sages still vital to this day.